a modern approach to business english

The Bobbs-Merrill Business Education Series:
Series Editor: Verleigh Ernest

A Modern Approach to Business English / *Annie DeCaprio*
A Modern Approach to Business Spelling / *Annie DeCaprio*
Basic Accounting, Second Edition / *Calvin Engler*
Business Correspondence / *Waldo C. Wright*
Business English: A Worktext with Programed Reinforcement / *Donald A. Sheff*
Business Spelling and Word Power / *A. H. Lass*
Career Builder Business Management Case Studies
Career Builder Secretarial Case Studies
Principles of Landmark abc Shorthand, Series I
Principles of Landmark abc Shorthand Workbook, Series I
ABC Shorthand Dictation and Transcription, Landmark Edition, Series I / *Jordan Hale*
Theory Tapes for Landmark abc Shorthand, Series I
Principles of ABC Shorthand, Landmark Edition, Series II
ABC Shorthand Workbook, Landmark Edition, Series II
ABC Shorthand Dictation and Transcription, Landmark Edition, Series II
ABC Shorthand Dictionary, Landmark Edition
Theory Tapes for Principles of ABC Shorthand, Landmark Edition, Series II
Typing: College Edition / *Verleigh Ernest*
Typing Power—Spelling Power, Volume One / *Norman Elliott, Rose Palmer, Steve Rosen*

ANNIE DeCAPRIO

a modern approach to business english

Bobbs-Merrill Educational Publishing
Indianapolis

A Modern Approach to Business English

Copyright © 1973 by ITT Educational Services, Inc.
Printed in the United States of America
All rights reserved. No part of this book shall be reproduced or transmitted in any form or by any means, electronic or mechanical, including photocopying, recording, or by any information or retrieval system, without written permission from the Publisher:

The Bobbs-Merrill Company, Inc.
4300 West 62nd Street
Indianapolis, Indiana 46268

First Edition
Fourth Printing—1977
Library of Congress Catalog Card Number: 73-90044
ISBN 0-672-96102-4 (pbk)

name section date

UNIT 1

sentences and sentence fragments (1)

Introduction

A sentence has two parts: A subject, which tells us whom or what we are talking about, and a predicate, which tells us what the subject does.

John speaks.

This is a sentence. It expresses a complete thought by telling us who (*John,* the subject) does what (*speaks,* the predicate). Here is another complete sentence:

Tall, handsome **John speaks.**

We have merely added some words that describe our subject. They do not change the subject. The subject is still *John,* and the predicate is still *speaks.* Here is another sentence:

Tall, handsome **John speaks** *with fluency.*

Tall, handsome describes *John. With fluency* describes *speaks.*
    Use this approach whenever you want to find the subject and the predicate of a sentence. Ask who or what is the doer of the action and what does the subject do.
    To find the subject of a sentence that is a question, you will often have to rearrange the words: *Does John speak?* becomes *John does speak.* The predicate of this sentence is *does speak.*
    A sentence that begins with *there* can also be rearranged to make it easier to find the subject and the predicate: *There* **is John** becomes **John is** *there. John* is the subject. *Is* is the predicate.
    Note that the predicate may be made up of more than one word:

John has been speaking *for some time.*

Again the subject is *John.* The predicate is *has been speaking.*
    When dealing with a long sentence, a frequent mistake is to write only part of the sentence as though it were a complete sentence.

Page 1

Tall, handsome **John,** *president of our club since 1971.* **Was invited** *to speak at some length at the meeting held on Monday.*

The first fragment tells us who, but it does not tell us what he does. If you cannot find both a subject and a predicate, you may be reading not a sentence, but a sentence fragment.

There is another type of sentence fragment of which you should be wary. This is the fragment that apparently contains both a subject and a predicate but does not express a complete thought. For example:

John, *running at full speed.*

The subject is *John*. The apparent predicate is *running*. But the words do not express a complete thought. It does not answer the question, *John, running at full speed*, did what? The fragment could be made into one of these two complete sentences: **John was running** *at full speed;* or **John,** *running at full speed,* **fell.**

In this unit, we shall look at some complete sentences and learn to recognize sentence fragments so that they can be avoided.

Subjects and Predicates

A. Decide on the subject and predicate of each sentence below. Underline the subject with one line. Underline the predicate with two.

EXAMPLES: The manager works with diligence and initiative.

On Wednesday evening after the banquet, the executives will meet.

The secretary, after taking dictation, transcribed her notes.

1. Mr. Marco is here.
2. There are no women in executive positions.
3. Have you seen any women in executive positions?
4. I like this book.
5. This book has been sold to over 200,000 readers.
6. These readers have uniformly expressed their delight with this book.
7. Did you enjoy the book?
8. Have you seen the president and his cabinet in session?
9. There is a simple solution to the problem of unfulfilled obligations.
10. Is there any way to solve this problem?
11. Able, efficient Mary types with speed and accuracy.
12. The foreman spoke with authority and directness.
13. On Tuesday morning after the coffee break the department heads met.
14. Mr. Jones, after giving dictation, dismissed his secretary.
15. No one, in my opinion, can deliver a better sales talk than Mrs. Reynolds.
16. Modern and functional are our new office desks.
17. The men will arrive before noon.
18. Near him sat the two partners of the firm.
19. Economy is less needed than efficiency.
20. A strong America is the objective of our government.

UNIT 1

sentences and sentence fragments (2)

Compound Subjects and Predicates

When the subject is composed of two or more items, it is called a *compound subject*.

John and **George** spoke.   Both **Mr. Castro** and **Mr. Moore** were present.

A. Underline the compound subject in each sentence.

EXAMPLE: <u>George and Harry</u> are co-owners of the restaurant.

1. Orders and receipts are filed separately.
2. Mr. Roberts and Mr. Jones are in their office.
3. At the stroke of noon, the president and his cabinet met in the east wing.
4. Bill and Herbert do not get along well together.
5. Neither Mr. Black nor Mr. Green has sent in his reply.
6. Both men and women can wear this hair style.
7. The receipts and invoices are kept in this file cabinet.
8. The accountant and the lawyer were waiting at the airport.
9. Cities and rural communities differ in their traffic patterns.
10. The letters and packages are ready to take to the mail room.

A compound predicate consists of two verbs joined by *and* or a similar word.

John **rose** and **addressed** the meeting.

B. Draw two lines under the compound predicate in each sentence.

1. The secretary has transcribed her notes and mailed the letter.
2. He cleaned and cooked the fish that he caught in the brook.
3. She can type and file expertly.

Page 3

4. There is and has always been a planet earth.
5. Is there now or has there ever been a lid for this pan?
6. Salaries in our firm rose last year and then leveled off.
7. The men will arise early and depart for the camp at the appointed hour.
8. The executive cancelled one appointment and made another.
9. The builders have excavated the basement and laid the foundations.
10. Has the report been examined and approved?

Subjects in Sentences That Are Commands

In a command, the subject (*you*) is not stated, but it is understood.

> **Mail** the letter.

The addition of the subject would make this sentence: *You mail the letter.*

A. In the following sentences, draw a line under the subjects. Draw two lines under the predicates. If the sentence is a command write *U* after it to indicate that the subject is understood.

1. Sue and Mary typed and filed constantly all morning.
2. Avoid erasures on typed material.
3. Where am I?
4. Report to your supervisor before lunch.
5. We wish to see either Miss White or Miss Brown.
6. Neither of them is here.
7. Before him stood New York with its towering buildings, shimmering rivers, and bridges.
8. Give it to me this minute.
9. Waiting at the airport were the accountant and the lawyer.
10. There are more than 50 percent of the offices rented.
11. Near him sat the two partners of the firm.
12. These are but some of our needs.
13. Clearly, the technological revolution has not ended.
14. We need a fast, maneuverable helicopter gun-ship and an improved anti-aircraft weapon.
15. He and his family arrived by car while the moving van was still en route.
16. On the second morning, he heard the phone ring and then a one-sided conversation.
17. A neighbor, a fellow worker, came to welcome him and his family.
18. The pickup truck skidded on the patch of ice and careened into the ditch.
19. Tens of thousands of people from coast to coast are now making money in this way.
20. Consider the unique experience of our company which has researched this subject.

UNIT 1

sentences and sentence fragments (3)

Sentence Fragments

A. Write *C* after each complete sentence. If the words do not contain both a subject and a predicate and if the subject is not understood, as in a command, write *F* for sentence fragment.

1. Running down the street at full speed. _____
2. We agree. _____
3. Night after night, day after day, until he could hardly speak anymore. _____
4. Mr. Roberts, the most noted authority on aerodynamics in recent years. _____
5. Furtively looking up and down the street, then darting to safety, he escaped. _____
6. Where are we going? _____
7. Nearing the attainment of the production goals set at our last meeting. _____
8. Nearly everyone was present, including the president and his aides. _____
9. Nearly everyone present, including the president and his aides. _____
10. There is no time for further discussion. _____

One kind of sentence fragment results when the writer mistakes a dependent clause for an independent clause. An example of this is:

> *Since the order arrived.*

The word *since* limits our thought in such a manner that it does not express a complete thought although it contains a subject, *order*, and a predicate, *arrived*. Something must be added to complete the thought:

> *Since the order arrived, we have made headway.*

In this sentence, *we have made headway* is one clause. *Since the order arrived* is another clause. Because *we have made headway* could stand as a sentence by itself, it is called an independent clause. Because *since the order arrived* could not stand by itself, it is called a dependent clause.

Page 5

B. After each sentence below, write *D* if the underlined words constitute a dependent clause. Write *I* if the underlined words constitute an independent clause. Write *N* if the words do not constitute a clause.

1. I prefer the typewriter <u>on the table</u>. _____
2. <u>When a letter is typed</u>, it represents the firm. _____
3. He led his sales force <u>because of his ambition</u>. _____
4. <u>Because he was ambitious</u>, he soon impressed his employers. _____
5. <u>We can offer this guarantee</u> because of our high quality control. _____
6. <u>Standing behind each man</u> is a woman who prods him into action. _____
7. <u>She is a fine bookkeeper</u> because she is quick with figures. _____
8. <u>Although we have worked hard</u>, the end is not yet in sight. _____
9. <u>Your order was received in time</u> despite an unexpected delay. _____
10. Because we have years of experience, <u>we can do the best job</u>. _____

Simple and Complex Sentences

A simple sentence is a sentence composed of one independent clause.

> We have made headway.

A complex sentence is a sentence composed of an independent clause and a dependent clause.

> Since the order arrived, we have made headway.

A. Write *S* after each sentence that is a simple sentence. Write *C* if it is a complex sentence. Write *F* if it is a sentence fragment.

1. On the last day in April we will hold our meeting. _____
2. Despite our protests, he entered the primary race for the Senate. _____
3. We will expect delivery as soon as possible. _____
4. After they deliver the goods, we will bill them. _____
5. If anything ever sounded as though it were unwise. _____
6. Please try to arrive before 10 o'clock to avoid any delay. _____
7. Though you have a prior engagement, won't you try to attend? _____
8. There are several good reasons for our decision and for our unwillingness to participate. _____
9. The merchandise arrived in damaged condition despite the warnings we sent you. _____
10. Don't you agree with the Commission's report on unemployment? _____

name　　　　　　　　　　　section　　　　　　　　　　　　date

UNIT 1

sentences and sentence fragments (4)

assignment

A. In creating copy for advertising, copywriters occasionally take liberties with the strict rules of grammar in order to attract attention. The following piece of advertising copy makes deliberate use of sentence fragments. Underline each sentence fragment that you find.

I FEEL LIKE I'M GIVING A PARTY

Our chain of restaurants has hired thousands of waitresses.
Since 1960.
So let us tell you something about our girls. Makeup can change a face, but it can't change the girl. A waitress has to have a special attitude. If she does, you get that special service. If she doesn't, we both pay.
Sandy Wilson is 22. She's from Syracuse, New York. And after one year on the job, this is what she told us about being a waitress:
"At first I was bashful.
Then people began thanking me for an enjoyable meal.
I liked that. I realized how much I wanted everything to go just right.
Then I had fun when they did."
We're combing America for more girls like Sandy Wilson. As soon as we meet them, we promise to introduce them to you.
Girls who bring a little something extra to their job. That's the Food Shoppe way.

　　　　　　　　　　　　　　　　　　　　　　　　　　The Food Shoppes

B. Underline the dependent clauses in the following paragraphs.

Since an automobile is one of the most expensive purchases many of us ever make, <u>when buying a car</u> you would be wise to shop carefully, comparing prices and finance terms. Remember <u>that when shopping for means to finance your car, you have a right to know the effective annual rate of interest</u>, and the person <u>from whom you get the contract</u> is legally obliged to tell you.

Consider the advantages and disadvantages of buying a new car as opposed to a used car. <u>When you buy a used car</u>, other drivers have had experience with the model. You can avoid models <u>that you know have defects</u>. An advantage of a new car is the manufacturer's warranty, but read yours carefully <u>to see what it covers</u>.

Despite the large amount of money <u>that is involved</u>, many people know less about the car <u>they buy</u> than about many less expensive items <u>that they purchase</u>.

C. In each sentence, underline the subject of the independent clause.

<u>Keeping a car in good condition</u> is a wise investment. If you read the owner's manual, <u>you</u> will find the information you need in order to do so.

Proper maintenance is the least expensive aspect of car ownership. It is less than the cost of oil and gas, less than the cost of insurance, and it may even be less than the interest on your installment loan.

Here are some of the things on your car that should be checked daily: The windshield, mirrors, and windows should be clean. The windshield wipers and washer should be operating efficiently. The temperature gauge and the oil pressure gauge should be checked frequently while driving. If the oil pressure is low, you should stop at the nearest service station to prevent damage to the engine. If the temperature gauge is high, damage can also result.

The brakes should be checked while you are driving. When traffic conditions permit, they should be checked by stepping hard on the pedal. A feeling of sponginess is an indication that you need the help of a repairman. Your owner's manual will tell you how often to change the oil. While the headlights, brake lights, and turn signals are on, you can walk around the car to make sure that all of them are working.

Does your state have a motor vehicle inspection? If so, you will know that your headlights are properly adjusted after you take the test. Then the car can be stationed in front of a wall while you note the place where the correctly adjusted beam is reflected. You can continue to use the wall as a way of checking the headlights.

A properly maintained car is not only a good investment, it may save your life.

UNIT 2
run-on sentences; agreement of subjects and predicates (1)

Introduction

A run-on sentence results when two sentences are punctuated as if they were one:

> We hope to attend the banquet, we may be detained by business.

The writer often makes this mistake because he recognizes that the two sentences are closely related in meaning. A comma as in the above sentence, however, is not enough to connect the two sentences. The words *and, or,* and *but* after the comma will furnish the necessary connection:

> We hope to attend the banquet, but we may be detained by business.

Another way in which closely related sentences can be connected is with a semicolon:

> *Thank you for your note; it was most timely.*

And, or, and *but* are called conjunctions, and, as we will see in the unit on conjunctions, there are many more (*so, therefore, then,* for example). For the purposes of remedying run-on sentences, however, we will use only the three most common conjunctions.

In addition to the run-on sentence, this unit deals with agreement between subject and predicate. Although you would never answer the phone by saying *Mr. Smith are here,* when sentences become more complicated, it is easy to fall into the trap of writing a singular subject with a plural predicate. Make sure you know the subject of your sentence when writing the predicate:

> One **man** in the firm of hundreds **is** to be honored.

In this example sentence, although *is* follows *hundreds,* the subject of the sentence is singular, *man,* and that is the word with which the predicate must agree.

When a sentence contains two or more subjects connected by *and,* the predicate should be plural:

> **Jack and Jill are** *going up the hill.*

When both subjects refer to one thing or one person, on the other hand, a singular predicate follows. If, for example, one man fills the office of both secretary and treasurer:

> **The treasurer and secretary is** *here.*

If the positions are held by two different men, the general rule applies:

> **The treasurer and secretary are** *here.*

A few words are so closely connected that they are considered one unit:

> **Ham and eggs is** *my favorite dish.*

But

> **Ham and eggs are** *on my shopping list.*

When two subjects are connected by *or* or *nor,* make the predicate agree with the subject that is closest to it:

> *Jack or* **Jill is** *going up the hill.*   *Neither the workers nor* **the manager was** *pleased with the plan.*

As a general rule of business usage, however, note that the subjects would actually be transposed in the last of the above sentences:

> *Neither the manager nor* **the workers were** *pleased with the plan.*

That is, when one subject is singular and one is plural, it is generally smoother writing to place the plural subject last, closer to the predicate.

UNIT 2

run-on sentences; agreement of subjects and predicates (2)

Commas in Sentences That Have Been Combined

Very short sentences can be connected and made one merely by adding *and, or,* and *but.* If the sentence is short, a comma is not necessary:

> He washed the dishes and she dried them.

Most sentences, however, require a comma to alert the reader to expect another complete independent clause:

> *After a long argument he agreed to wash the dishes, and she cooperated to the extent of drying them.*

A. Add commas to the following sentences if you decide they are necessary.

1. Come and see me.
2. We were pleased to receive your order and we are happy to comply.
3. We shall expedite the adjustment and put your order into work quickly.
4. Both Mr. Jones and I shall look forward to serving you.
5. The production department has been very slow and we are also having trouble with shipping.
6. The plant has received the new machines and we will be ready to go into production shortly.
7. I will be in Milwaukee next week and I hope to see you there.
8. Please note the many errors in this letter and correct them.
9. The doctor examined the patient and he declared that surgery was necessary.
10. Spring is here and the birds are singing.
11. The weather remained calm and on the fourth day the explorers set out.
12. The drilling went faster and more accurately than many experts expected and every well had been extinguished.
13. Choose firm, level chairs or sofas to sit on and adjust your automobile seat closer to the steering wheel, tilting it as nearly upright as you can.
14. The formula sounds so simple that it will be hard for you to believe it.

15. A slumping figure betrays advancing age and nothing signals a depressed person more surely than a defeated slouch.
16. Some people stand and walk with their feet pointing outward instead of parallel.
17. Kneecaps should turn out slightly and feet should point straight ahead.
18. Learn the correct form and practice it.
19. Shoulder slump causes muscles to become tight in the chest and front of the neck.
20. A good posture helps your appearance and your health.

Sentence Fragments and Run-on Sentences

A. Some of the expressions below are correct, complete sentences. Some are sentence fragments, and some are run-on sentences. Write *C* after correct sentences. Write *F* after sentence fragments. Write *R* after run-on sentences.

1. Whenever the attorney had a chance to speak. _____
2. Ship the books, we will remit within 30 days. _____
3. Lessons by day, study at night. _____
4. Because of his initiative, and because he had the proper connections. _____
5. What will happen next? _____
6. Continue with your college course, you will graduate at the head of your class. _____
7. Looking around, sizing up the situation, and foretelling all its ramifications. _____
8. Oil, steel, and coal in the right proportions. _____
9. Expect only big things of yourself, and never waver nor doubt that they will come true. _____
10. Though Miss Blake is young, she is not immature, so I am convinced she can handle the job. _____
11. Speaking of telephone prices. A new low rate for evening calls is now in practice. _____
12. Carbon copies are important for checking data, especially in business correspondence. ____
13. Stay late tonight, you will be paid for overtime. _____
14. Please check your accuracy, however speed is essential too. _____
15. Of course we are interested, you would be too. _____
16. We have written twice, please reply at once. _____
17. As soon as the incident was reported, rumors started flying; accordingly, the President rushed to clarify the issues to the nation. _____
18. Courtesy is contagious, therefore smile often. _____
19. Help! _____
20. We followed the directions, but we couldn't assemble the instrument no matter how many different ways we attempted to arrange the elements. _____

UNIT 2

run-on sentences; agreement of subjects and predicates (3)

Agreement of Subject and Predicate

When any of the following words are the subject of a sentence, the predicate should be singular: *each, anyone, anybody, someone, somebody, everyone, everybody,* and *nobody.*

Nobody wants *to make grammatical mistakes.*

Disregard expressions beginning with *as well as, together with, in addition to, accompanied by,* and so forth when deciding on the subject. These expressions give incidental information which could be omitted. They do not change the subject.

Mr. Jones, *as well as Mr. Smith,* **is** *coming to the convention.*

A. In the space provided, write the correct form of the word in parentheses.

1. Each order (has, have) been received. _____
2. Each of the orders (has, have) been received. _____
3. Nobody among the secretaries (seem, seems) capable of supervising tests. _____
4. My boss, together with his assistant, (was, were) able to attend the convention. _____
5. Mr. Jones, together with his wife, (is, are) planning to take a holiday. _____
6. A series of changes in office routines (is, are) expected soon. _____
7. News of the price decreases (has, have) reached the customers. _____
8. Six tons of coal (was, were) paid for on the last bill. _____
9. The number of marriages in the firm (is, are) increasing. _____
10. A number of filing clerks and secretaries (has, have) applied. _____

When a quantity is measured in one lump sum, it should be treated as though it were one item:

> **Five tons is** *a lot of coal.*   **Eighty miles an hour is** *too fast.*

When deciding on the predicate that the subject *number* takes, use this rule: When it is preceded by *the*, it takes a singular predicate; when preceded by any other word, including *a*, it takes a plural predicate:

> **The** *number of failures* **is** *low.*   **A** *number of people* **have** *failed.*

Titles of books with plurals in them are nevertheless the title of only one book.

> **"Business Letters" is** *a fine book.*

Committee, jury, class, crowd, and similar words may be either singular or plural. When the group they refer to acts as a single unit, use a singular predicate. When the sentence is about the individuals who make up the group, use a plural predicate.

> *The* **committee were** *arguing.*   *The* **committee is** *ready to vote.*

B. Underline the correct word in each sentence. Write *S* if it is singular; write *P* if it is plural.

1. "Writing Better Letters" (is, are) a good book for secretaries. _____
2. "Ideas on Office Improvement" (was, were) put aside for the new typist. _____
3. The committee (has, have) decided to issue their report next week. _____
4. The jury (was, were) asked by the judge to render its decision. _____
5. The faculty of the school (seem, seems) to be against new proposals. _____

Although *committee are* and *crowd are* are correct in some sentences, many writers would make the sentences with such subjects less awkward by writing:

> *The members of the committee are arguing.*   *The people in the crowd are angry.*

The name of a firm often includes the names of more than one person, as well as the word *Company.* You must decide how the word is used in the sentence to decide whether company names are being used in a singular or plural sense:

> *Merrill Lynch, Pierce, Fenner and Smith was America's largest brokerage house.*

run-on sentences; agreement of subjects and predicates (4)

Agreement of Subject and Predicate

A. Underline the correct word in parentheses in each sentence. (Whether *none* is singular or plural depends on its meaning in the sentence.)

1. Each order (has, have) been processed.
2. Each of the orders (has, have) been processed.
3. Anyone (know, knows) what the solution should be.
4. Walter Clark of Chicago, as well as his entire family, (intend, intends) to spend his summer here.
5. Either Mr. Burns or Mr. Jones (is, are) the logical candidate.
6. There (is, are) a table and a lamp still unshipped.
7. One million dollars (is, are) a lot of money.
8. We feel that neither your office nor your plants (is, are) adequately equipped.
9. The committee (has, have) issued a final decree.
10. Each of the children, in addition to his parents, (is, are) entitled to a free pass.
11. A number of photos (were, was) taken.
12. Anybody with a sound mind (are, is) eligible to enter.
13. I feel that politics (has, have) entered a decade of turmoil.
14. The number of books available for sale (are, is) low.
15. Thirty-six percent of our total production (has, have) been sold.
16. None of the suppliers (has, have) called since our orders were sent.
17. Hundreds of teachers, together with their students, (hail, hails) our product.
18. Measles (is, are) a contagious disease.
19. This series of figures (is, are) much too confusing.
20. Here (is, are) the list of figures you requested.

Review of Unit 2

A. After each sentence, copy the subject of the sentence. Write *S* if the subject is singular. Write *P* if the subject is plural.

1. A man called at your office. _____
2. A tall, dark, handsome, cultured man called at your office. _____
3. Frank and Mary are staying overtime today. _____
4. Macy's and Gimbel's are friendly competitors. _____
5. Efficient supervisors and executives have always been at a premium. _____
6. Both the designer and the engineer seem competent workers. _____
7. Peaches and cream is my favorite breakfast dish. _____
8. A supervisor for all receptionists must be picked today. _____
9. Bread and butter is a staple in the American diet. _____
10. Office machinery must be covered and carefully protected. _____

B. Underline the subject in each sentence in the following letter with one underline. Underline each predicate twice.

Gentlemen:

In your recent letter you ordered several items for immediate delivery. Our production manager and our consulting engineer have informed me of some delays in retooling machines for your order. We shall expedite this adjustment and put your order into work quickly. The shipping department will, of course, inform you of the shipping date, and Mr. Jones will visit you personally if necessary. Please understand our problems in retooling and accept our assurance of careful attention. Botl Mr. Jones and I shall look forward to serving you.

Sincerely,

Double the final consonant of a word before adding a suffix if:
1. **the last syllable of the word has the consonant-vowel-consonant pattern of *pin***
2. **the accent is on the last syllable (*occur*)**
3. **the suffix begins with a vowel (*occurred*)**

UNIT 2
run-on sentences; agreement of subjects and predicates (5)

assignment

A. Rewrite the letter below. Eliminate sentence fragments and run-on sentences.

Dear Mr. White:

    No two men are alike, one man jumps to a conclusion without careful consideration of all available information. Another man examines each fact. Checks every claim. And profits from the experience of others, then he makes his decision.
    We believe you are the latter type of purchaser. The man who has to see for himself before he buys. For this reason we are delighted to offer you this electric razor on a free-home-trial basis. Although you may have used another razor all your life. After seven days with it you will never again want to switch back to your old-type razor.
    So mail the enclosed card today, we will ship your sample razor by return post.

                                  Sincerely,

B. Cross out the incorrect punctuation and incorrect words in the following letter. Mark a caret and write the punctuation correctly above the errors. Use this symbol to indicate a comma: ∧ Use this symbol to indicate a period: ⊙ Follow the example:

We regret that you have failed to receive your order, ~~we~~ ⊙ We are taking steps to fill it immediately. Fortunately∧ shipping conditions have improved.

Dear Mr. Jones:

On looking over our records this week, we find that each of your offices has failed to renew its subscription to "Modern Times." And we assure you we regret this very much. Each of our previous letters express our appreciation of having you as a subscriber. And explain to you our desire to have all your offices remain as regular subscribers.

Everyone on our staff are concerned over your failure to renew, was this failure due to something that somebody in my office have said or done? We would be very much pleased to hear any suggestions you may have, and assure you that we will take all steps possible to remedy any unfortunate situation.

You know "Modern Times" are the finest magazine in its field, whether drama, science, current events, or politics are your interest, "Modern Times" have articles of interest to you. "Modern Times" is read and enjoyed by men in all walks of life, it is read by doctors, it is read by lawyers, it is read by engineers, the list of readers are just endless.

We do hope that you will reconsider and forward your renewal so that we may again enter your name on our list of subscribers and friends. After all, are there anything more important than loyal friends?

                Sincerely yours,

name section date

UNIT 3

nouns and their plurals (1)

Introduction

Nouns are used to name persons, places, things, or abstract qualities. Here are some examples:

>Nouns that name persons: *man, typist, Smith*
>Nouns that name places: *courtroom, school, lake*
>Nouns that name things: *chair, shorthand, book*
>Nouns that name abstract qualities: *truth, initiative, readiness*

A proper noun is a specific name: *John, America, Buick.* Other nouns are called common nouns: *boy, country, car.*

Most nouns, of course, form the plural by adding *-s* or *-es*. The best way to be sure of forming the correct plural for nouns other than those that add *-s* or *-es* is to look them up in the dictionary. We can, however, give you a few rules for forming the less common plurals, and that is what this unit will do.

Plurals Formed by Adding -s and -es

A. Write the plural forms of these words by adding -s.

1. cigarette _____
2. group _____
3. piece _____
4. Smith _____
5. apartment _____
6. crowd _____
7. European _____
8. receipt _____
9. truth _____
10. typewriter _____
11. desk _____
12. paper _____
13. town _____
14. automobile _____
15. pen _____

Words that end in -s, -sh, -z, -ch, or -x add -es to form the plural.

B. Write the plural forms of these words by adding -es.

1. box _____
2. church _____
3. glass _____
4. tax _____
5. kiss _____
6. bus _____
7. wish _____
8. lash _____
9. rich _____
10. grass _____
11. bush _____
12. gas _____
13. lunch _____
14. bunch _____
15. quiz _____

Plurals of Words That End in -y

Words that end in a vowel followed by -y form the plural by adding -s. Words that end in a consonant followed by -y change the -y to -i and add -es.

A. Write the plural of each word.

EXAMPLES: alley   alleys   baby   babies

1. efficiency _____
2. daisy _____
3. country _____
4. play _____
5. county _____
6. alloy _____
7. essay _____
8. laboratory _____
9. survey _____
10. specialty _____
11. attorney _____
12. company _____
13. lady _____
14. valley _____
15. variety _____

Page 20   nouns and their plurals (1)

UNIT 3

nouns and their plurals (2)

Plurals of Words That End in -o

Use the following rules to help you keep in mind spellings of words that you have used. When you feel unsure, however, use your dictionary, because these rules are not completely reliable.

Words that end in -o preceded by a vowel (*cameo*) usually add -s to form the plural. Words that end in -o preceded by a consonant (*cargo*) usually add -es. Musical terms, however, usually add -s regardless of the preceding letter (for example, *concerto*).

A. Write the plurals. Use your dictionary to find the plurals of words you are unsure of. One word's plural form is not in agreement with the rules above.

EXAMPLES: embryo *embryos* ; hero *heroes*

1. solo _____
2. alto _____
3. ratio _____
4. Negro _____
5. veto _____

6. echo _____
7. portfolio _____
8. embargo _____
9. potato _____
10. auto _____

11. banjo _____
12. radio _____
13. motto _____
14. tomato _____
15. volcano _____

Words Ending in -f or -fe

If you do not know the plurals of words in this group, you must use your dictionary, for there is no rule telling when to change -f or -fe to -ves to form the plural and when to form the plural in the usual way (*loaves,* but *chefs*).

A. Write the plurals of these words.

1. calf _____
2. bailiff _____
3. leaf _____
4. shelf _____
5. roof _____

6. half _____
7. chief _____
8. life _____
9. thief _____
10. plaintiff _____

11. knife _____
12. dwarf _____
13. self _____
14. wife _____
15. safe _____

Irregular Plurals

A few words are irregular, but are so common that you probably have no trouble with them.

A. Write the plurals of these words.

1. child _____
2. man _____
3. ox _____
4. foot _____
5. mouse _____
6. woman _____
7. gentleman _____
8. louse _____
9. tooth _____

Plurals of Some Words of Foreign Origin

A few words that were originally Latin or Greek words retain the plural forms that they had in the original language. They must be memorized. Some of these words have two permissible plurals, but one form is usually preferred.

A. Copy the plural forms of these words.

	Singular	*Plural*		*Singular*	*Plural*
1.	alumna	alumnae _____	8.	alumnus	alumni _____
2.	analysis	analyses _____	9.	antithesis	antitheses _____
3.	axis	axes _____	10.	basis	bases _____
4.	crisis	crises _____	11.	datum	data _____
5.	oasis	oases _____	12.	hypothesis	hypotheses _____
6.	parenthesis	parentheses _____	13.	phenomenon	phenomena _____
7.	synthesis	syntheses _____	14.	synopsis	synopses _____

B. Memorize the preferred spelling of the following words.

Singular	*Preferred Plural*	*Acceptable Plural*	*Singular*	*Preferred Plural*	*Acceptable Plural*
1. appendix	appendixes	appendices	4. criterion	criteria	criterions
2. formula	formulas	formulae	5. index	indexes	indices
3. medium	mediums	media	6. memorandum	memorandums	memoranda

Note that *media,* when it refers to channels of communication (television, radio, magazines, and so forth), is the plural form that is preferred.

UNIT 3

nouns and their plurals (3)

Plurals of Numerals, Letters, and Characters

The only time an apostrophe is used to form plurals occurs with numerals, letters, and characters (*9's*). Numerals that are written as a word form their plurals in the usual way (*nines*).

A. Make the following items plural.

1. 6 _____   3. 55 _____   5. h _____   7. + _____   9. = _____

2. abc _____   4. x _____   6. ¢ _____   8. 4 _____   10. w _____

Plurals of Titles

When writing to two people, modern usage requires giving each person his title: *Dear Mr. Smith and Mr. Jones.* A few companies prefer the older form, and use only one word, a plural, for both men. *Messrs.* is the plural of *Mr.*, and *Mmes.* is the plural of *Mrs.* (*Dear Messrs. Smith and Jones, Dear Mmes. Smith and Jones*). If you write to a firm in which three brothers are partners, you would not write *Dear Mr. Kern, Mr. Kern, and Mr. Kern,* however. That problem can be avoided by the use of the salutation *Gentlemen* or by the use of *Dear Messrs. Kern.* The plural of *Miss* is *Misses,* and the plural of *Dr.* is *Drs.* Again, however, modern usage prefers *Dear Miss Smith and Miss Jones* to *Dear Misses Smith and Jones,* and it prefers *Dear Dr. Smith and Dr. Jones.*

A. Write salutations of business letters to people named Smith and Jones as if they were the kinds of people after each number.

1. two unmarried women _____   3. two lawyers _____

2. two doctors _____   4. two married women _____

Words with the Same Singular and Plural Forms

A few words are written the same in the singular and plural forms. A few words look plural, but are always used with a singular meaning, and they must take a singular predicate **(politics is** a *vital field*). Your dictionary can tell you if a word is singular or plural.

A. Memorize these words that have the same singular and plural forms.

1. corps
2. means (method)
3. riches
4. deer
5. Japanese
6. goods
7. fish
8. series
9. trout
10. gross
11. sheep
12. grouse
13. head (of cattle)
14. elk
15. salmon

B. Learn these words that are always used in the singular.

1. aeronautics
2. ethics
3. measles
4. arthritis
5. logistics
6. news
7. civics
8. phonetics
9. rickets
10. economics
11. physics (the science)
12. politics

C. The following nouns are usually used in the plural.

1. acoustics
2. cattle
3. remains
4. annals
5. goods
6. scissors
7. barracks
8. pants
9. suds
10. belongings
11. proceeds
12. tactics

Plurals

A. Write the plural form of each of these nouns in the space provided.

1. book ─────────────
2. invoice ─────────────
3. office ─────────────
4. mass ─────────────
5. tax ─────────────
6. wife ─────────────
7. half ─────────────
8. chief ─────────────
9. plaintiff ─────────────
10. proof ─────────────
11. Mr. Hatch ─────────────
12. 26 ─────────────
13. twenty-six ─────────────
14. X ─────────────
15. series ─────────────

UNIT 3

nouns and their plurals (4)

A. Write the plurals of these words.

1. watch _____
2. receipt _____
3. company _____
4. self _____
5. datum _____
6. radio _____
7. stimulus _____
8. valley _____
9. alumnus _____
10. criterion _____

11. Mrs. _____
12. zero _____
13. letterhead _____
14. census _____
15. deletion _____
16. analysis _____
17. court-martial _____
18. piano _____
19. medium _____
20. bureau _____

21. scissors _____
22. agency _____
23. C.P.A. _____
24. Jones _____
25. spoonful _____
26. gas _____
27. Miss _____
28. if _____
29. five _____
30. Mr. _____

B. Cross out the incorrectly spelled nouns and write the correct forms above them.

Industrys of all sorts have flourished in the central vallies of the Acme Mountains. Each year, cargoes of tomatos and potatoes are shipped from the valleys in large quantities. The area is famous for its fine tobaccoes, which are bought by all the large cigar companys. In addition to these agricultural products the region has fine facilitys for steel foundrys and for the manufacture of radioes and pianoes. The Caseys', who are attornies and steel men, made fortunes in alloyes, datas for which came from their own formulaes.

Review of Sentences

A. Mark *C* if the expression is a complete sentence. Mark *F* if it is a sentence fragment. Mark *R* if it is a run-on sentence.

1. Early that month Lawrence, under an assumed name. _____
2. The two executives promised to see him eventually. _____
3. A government-financed campaign, assisted by the press. _____
4. The advantage of that trail is that it is short, it is possible to make the hike in one day. _____
5. In our relations with foreign governments, let us not be irrevocably committed. _____
6. A hospital stay in New York, like a stay in a hospital in New Jersey. _____
7. It is a serious problem, few people have found a solution for it. _____
8. Our company offers budget-cost plans to help with hospital and doctor bills. _____
9. The outcry was instantaneous, lobbyists immediately got in touch with their congressmen. _____
10. Currently, to curb or cure various diseases in order to diminish suffering. _____
11. Today the potential cure rate for cancer is better than two thirds. _____
12. The generation gap is very wide at the moment. _____
13. The average household makes approximately 5.5 calls a day, this is greater than it was a decade ago. _____
14. Three things distinguish rock music—the beat, the creativity, and the loudness. _____
15. His most important achievement goes much deeper, he has changed public attitudes. _____
16. Five presidents asked Congress to eliminate the USDA payments. _____
17. Today 80 percent of patients with advanced Hodgkin's disease, which starts in the lymph nodes and then spreads. _____
18. The medical profession is cooperating fully. _____
19. As scary as lightning is, it rarely strikes people, in fact, storms are a beautiful experience to outdoorsmen. _____
20. More to be feared than lightning by the hiker, sunburn and sore feet are worse. _____

UNIT 3
nouns and their plurals (5)

A. Choose the proper predicate in each sentence and write it on the line.

1. The data (has, have) been entered in the account book. _____
2. Our most successful media (is, are) radio and TV. _____
3. Our curriculum (include, includes) courses in many fields. _____
4. The bases for my contention (is, are) twofold. _____
5. (Were, was) the memoranda left on my desk? _____
6. The alumni (is, are) fully behind the dean. _____
7. The stimulus (has, have) been measured in electrical units. _____
8. The fathers-in-law (has, have) met for the first time. _____
9. The crisis in his illness (is, are) finally past. _____
10. The series of revisions (is, are) complete at last. _____
11. Riches (is, are) something to be thankful for. _____
12. Proper ethics (was, were) the backbone of the new concern. _____
13. What (are, is) the major criterion in judging a letter? _____
14. The theses the philosopher expounded (was, were) stimulating. _____
15. How many international crises (has, have) there been lately? _____
16. The latest phenomena in the electronics industry (seems, seem) to be concerned with transistors. _____
17. Three handfuls of rice (was, were) thrown at the couple. _____
18. What new formulae (were, was) presented by him? _____
19. Parentheses (present, presents) occasional punctuation problems. _____
20. An editor realizes that plot synopses (is, are) important. _____

B. Some of the words on this page are singular. Others are plural. Put a check in the appropriate column. If the word has no singular or no plural, leave the space beside the checked column blank. Otherwise, write the opposite form in the column you did not check.

	Singular	Plural
1. test		
2. column		
3. lighters		
4. children		
5. ladies		
6. attorney		
7. knife		
8. shelves		
9. phenomenon		
10. alumnus		
11. datum		
12. alloys		
13. volcanoes		
14. cupful		
15. brother-in-law		
16. species		
17. sheep		
18. politics		
19. zero		
20. company		
21. media		
22. spoonfuls		
23. criteria		
24. series		
25. mottoes		
26. contralto		
27. indexes		
28. appendixes		
29. civics		
30. memorandums		

Page 28   nouns and their plurals (5)

UNIT 4
possessive nouns (1)

Introduction

A possessive noun is one that shows ownership, authorship, or origin:

The company's factory (ownership)   *Shakespeare's play* (authorship)   *The lamp's glow* (origin)

Modern rules for forming the possessives are actually quite simple: Whether a noun is singular or plural, if it does not end in *-s*, form the possessive by adding apostrophe and *-s*.

box's   children's   company's   men's

Whether the noun is singular or plural, if it already ends in *s*, add only an apostrophe.

boxes'   Charles'   Mr. Woods'   companies'

Just as an apostrophe in a contraction reminds us that letters have been left out, the apostrophe in a possessive should remind you that words have been left out and rearranged. That is, the phrases above could be written:

*The factory of the company   The play of Shakespeare
The glow of the lamp*

Since, in these phrases, none of the words above end in *-s*, you know that when forming possessive nouns of the nouns at the end of the *of* phrase, you should add apostrophe plus *-s*. If the word at the end of the *of* phrase already ended in *-s*, as in

The factories of the companies   The home of Mr. Woods   The glow of the lamps

you would add only an apostrophe:

*The companies' factories   Mr. Woods' home
The lamps' glow*

Generally, preferred usage is to avoid using the possessive noun when the noun names an inanimate object, and in that case, the *of* phrase is used instead:

The architecture of the building   The roar of the airplane

Page 29

A few expressions that do use the possessive noun have been in the language for some time, and they are exceptions to this rule:

a stone's throw   a hair's breadth   at arm's length

Note that the rule applies to objects, not abstract qualities. *Truth's, times'*, and so forth are considered good usage.

Be particularly alert to the need for the apostrophe in expressions of time:

*in two weeks' time   a moment's hesitation
four hours' delay*

The Possessive Form Showing Joint Ownership

Sometimes you want to show possession of something that is jointly owned or authored. In this case, only the last noun is made possessive:

Gilbert and Sullivan's operetta   Smith and Miller's firm   John and Bill's vacation plans

It is important, of course, that you know whether possession is separate or joint. For example, *Chicago's and New York's police forces are among the finest*—here the context shows that the police forces are separate.

A. Rewrite the following words and phrases so that the possessive noun is used.

1. the clothes of the ladies _____
2. the ties of the men _____
3. the books of the boy _____
4. the wool of the sheep _____
5. the report of the boss _____
6. the meeting of the directors _____
7. the statement of the Vice-Presidents _____
8. the poetry of Burns _____
9. the finances of the firm _____
10. the letters of the secretaries _____
11. the store of John _____
12. the association of the teachers _____
13. the accounts of Levy and Jones _____
14. the musical by Rodgers and Hammerstein _____
15. the book by Johnson and Johnson _____

possessive nouns (1)

UNIT 4

possessive nouns (2)

The Possessive Forms of Compound Words and Abbreviations

To write the possessive form of an abbreviation, place the apostrophe and -s after the final period.

>　　*The U.S.A.'s tariff　　The U.N.'s policy*
>　　　　*John D. Rockefeller, Jr.'s money*

To form the possessive of a compound noun, place the apostrophe and -s after the last word in the noun. If the compound noun is hyphenated, this may mean that it has two final -s's: one on the first word making it plural, one on the last word making it possessive:

>　　*My brother-in-law's inheritance　　My brothers-in-law's*
>　　　　*inheritance*

A. The following sentences contain errors involving possessive nouns. Cross out the improperly spelled noun and write it correctly.

1. At the sales meeting it was agreed that new desks should be installed in the salesmens office. _____
2. Yesterdays techniques cannot succeed in todays market. _____
3. You have one weeks time to accept or reject this companys offer. _____
4. The managers, at last Wednesdays meeting, agreed to rebuild the executives recreation hall.

5. The new sales managers plan was discussed at the boards last meeting. _____
6. Roberts trouble is that he takes nobodys advice. _____
7. We agree with Mr. Johnsons plan for improving our office forces morale. _____
8. We asked Charles opinion, but he refused to discuss Smiths plan. _____
9. Miller and Jones is one of the citys finest firms. _____
10. Miller and Jones policies are in complete agreement with the District Attorneys suggested code of conduct. _____
11. Browns and Whites stores compete in the ladies garments line. _____
12. Green and Blacks store handles a complete line of mens items. _____

Page 31

13. A committee to support the U.S.s policy in Europe sent a flood of telegrams to Senator Bass office. _____

14. The A.A.A.s vehicle policy is under the I.C.C.s direction. _____

15. My sister-in-laws child left college after two years work. _____

Possessive Nouns and Appositions; Possessives in Names of Organizations

When an explanatory word or phrase follows a noun, only the last word in the phrase is made possessive:

> Smith, our salesman's, record is outstanding.
> Alexander the Great's conquests were vast.
> Chrysler, the automobile manufacturer's, main plants are in Michigan.

In such cases, the first noun is not made possessive.
   Often an organization will choose to omit the apostrophe from a plural noun in its title.

> The National **Farmers** Association   Columbia University **Teachers** College

When writing to such associations or companies, follow the form that appears on their letterhead.

A. Fill in the chart by adding the forms at the head of each column.

Singular	Singular Possessive	Plural	Plural Possessive
1. book			
2. child			
3. tax			
4. Smith & Smith			
5. wife			
6. ratio			
7. body			
8. criterion			
9. attorney			
10. workingman			
11. radio			
12. memorandum			
13. brother-in-law			
14. hero			
15. stockholder			

UNIT 4

possessive nouns (3)

The Plural and Possessive Forms

A. Fill in the chart by adding the forms at the head of each column.

Singular	Singular Possessive	Plural	Plural Possessive
1. roof			
2. journey			
3. letterhead			
4. committee			
5. county			
6. boss			
7. medium			
8. lady			
9. ox			
10. attorney general			

B. Rewrite the following phrases using the possessive form of the noun.

1. the home of Dickens _____
2. the editorials of the *New York Times* _____
3. the engine of the old bus _____
4. the daughter of my boss _____
5. the notes of the typists _____
6. the motor of the tape recorder _____

Page 33

Plural and Possessive Forms

A. Each of the following sentences contains one or more possessive nouns from which the apostrophe has been omitted. In the space provided, rewrite these possessive nouns correctly.

1. The chairmans report included details on the proposed workmens cafeteria. _____

2. The camp directors view was that drastic changes had to be made in Johns outlook. _____

3. Frederick the Wises policies are comparable to the fiscal policies of the Farmers National Alliance. _____

4. The sales managers convention dealt with the new organizations policies. _____

5. The Tribunes point of view is that a secretarys contributions sometimes exceed those of the employer. _____

B. Rewrite the following phrases using the possessive form of the noun.

1. the opinions of the attorneys-at-law _____
2. the women's page of the Detroit Daily News _____
3. the decision of the consuls general _____
4. the vote of the election committee _____
5. the argument of the committee members _____
6. the salesmen of Johnson and Johnson _____
7. the position of Mr. Castro _____
8. the relatives of my sisters-in-law _____
9. the sales record of Mr. Guinness _____
10. the policies of the companies _____

UNIT 4

possessive nouns (4)

A. Rewrite the following letter, using the possessive form of the noun instead of an *of* phrase wherever possible. (An *of* phrase does not *always* indicate possession.)

Dear Miss Consuela:

    This will acknowledge your letter of February 15. As I understand it, you and Mr. Wood would be willing to expand the manuscript of Mr. Wood. The understanding of Mr. Wood of the food technology field is such that the search of our publishing company to find an author competent in this field has ended. However, the writing competence of an author is not always equal to the technical competence of an author. For this reason, we hope you will undertake to work on the manuscript of Mr. Wood with him.
    Please send the outline of Mr. Wood. We would like to know exactly how the proposed book fits the demands of our market. As you know the ideas of editors-in-chief are not always the same as the ideas of authors, and we will have to have the okay of our editor-in-chief.
    Greetings of the season.

                                                Sincerely,

Review

A. Select the word in parentheses that fits the subject in each sentence.
Write the word beside the sentence.

1. Any number of consequences (is, are) possible. _____
2. Nearly one-third of our supply (has, have) been exhausted. _____
3. Mathematics as well as economics (is, are) required. _____
4. The members of the jury (is, are) in complete disagreement. _____
5. The jury and the judge, as well as the general public, (is, are) convinced of the
   defendant's innocence. _____

B. Write the predicate and subject number (singular or plural) below
each sentence.

1. Mr. Smith and his partner will speak at the meeting today.
   _____
2. Either Mary or her friends will be the best models for the new uniform.
   _____
3. Neither time nor effort should be spared in practicing typing.
   _____
4. Neither the desk nor the chairs have arrived at the office.
   _____
5. Each of the applicants has to fill out a questionnaire.
   _____
6. Any one of the export firms is able to handle the shipment.
   _____
7. Everybody in the sales force is asked to use the suggestion box.
   _____
8. Somebody in the executive office is responsible for time studies.
   _____
9. The news of the sales losses is coming over the ticker tape.
   _____
10. Each male and each female has equal opportunity for promotion.
    _____

possessive nouns (4)

name　　　　　　　　　　　　　section　　　　　　　　　　　　　date

UNIT 4

possessive nouns (5)

assignment

A. The following letter contains a number of errors in the use of possessive and plural nouns. Cross out each error and write the correct form above it.

Dear Reader:

In the worlds most famous museum, the Louvre in Paris, hangs a painting by Americas celebrated artist, James McNeill Whistler. This paintings formal title is "An Arrangement in Gray and Black," but it is better known by the simple name, "Whistlers Mother." Many studies have been made in an effort to explain the basises of this portraits almost universal appeal.

But what criterions can the art critic use in judging a painting? The critic is not like a scientist; he cannot set up a controlled experiment wherein a number of stimulus are shot into a subject and datums collected on the subjects reaction. No, the art critic must rely on his inner emotions and sensitivity when he analyzes a painting. His analyses of a painting is a very personal thing.

If you looked at "Whistlers Mother," what would you see? Would you recognize the source of this portraits greatness? Would you, like most of us, be left wondering what makes this painting a masterpiece?

Dr. Felix A. Richard has come forward to help you. Dr. Richards new book, *Art,* has just been published. For a limited period only, this fine book is being made available to you at a very special discount price.

In this books Table of Contents are listed such interesting topics as: Criterions of Evaluation; Mediums for Communicating Art to the Masses; The Artists Studio; The Analysis of Expression through Color.

After you have read this fine volume, you will find new meaning in such great works as "Whistlers Mother." New horizons of appreciation will be opened to you.

Send for your copy today. Don't delay. Make out your check and mail it at once.

　　　　　　　　　　　　　　　　　　　　　　　　Very truly yours,

B. Fill in the chart by adding the forms at the head of each column.

Singular	Singular Possessive	Plural	Plural Possessive
1. secretary			
2. employee			
3. notebook			
4. editor-in-chief			
5. woman			
6. mother-in-law			
7. Charles			
8. acoustics			
9. alumnus			
10. datum			
11. trousers			
12. captain			
13. crisis			
14. U.S.A.			
15. lady			

If English is not your native language, practice the forms of irregular past tenses: *bring, brought, brought; swim, swam, swum; drink, drank, drunk; blow, blew, blown.*

UNIT 5
pronouns (1)

Introduction

The pronoun is a shortcut by which you can save time and space. The pronoun can stand in a noun's place. Since many nouns are long words and most pronouns are short words, you can shorten statements by using pronouns skillfully.

Pronouns take different forms, depending upon how they are used in a sentence. You have used these different forms automatically for most of your life, so they probably do not cause you any difficulty now.

	Singular	*Plural*
First Person	I, me	we, us
Second Person	you	you
Third Person	he, she, it him, her	they, them

Possessive pronouns are unlike nouns in that they do not have an apostrophe. The possessive forms are:

	Singular	*Plural*
First Person	my, mine	our, ours
Second Person	your, yours	your, yours
Third Person	its, his, her, hers	their, theirs

The relative pronouns are *who, whom, which, that.*

> Here is the man **who** will be our next president.
> The book, **which** had fallen, was soon found.
> Shorthand is the subject **that** I like best.

This unit emphasizes the importance of agreement between the pronoun and the noun for which it stands. In the unit on sentences, we saw that the subject and verb of a sentence must agree in number (*boys are; man is*). Pronouns must agree with their antecedents in the same way. This can become tricky in a sentence like *England expects every man to do* **his** *duty,* yet if the writer will glance back to see what word the pronoun stands for (*man,* in this case), he will immediately select the pronoun's correct form (in this case, *his,* not *their*).

If a pronoun stands for two singular nouns connected by *and,* the pronoun should be plural (*Mr. Johnson and Miss Smith are on **their** way*). Note, however, that occasionally two nouns apply to only one person, and in this case the pronoun is singular. If one man is both secretary and treasurer, for example, this sentence would be correct: *The Secretary and Treasurer gave **his** report.*

When two antecedents are connected by *or* or *nor,* have the pronoun agree with the noun nearest to it (*Neither Johnson nor Smith knows **his** business*). When one antecedent is singular and the other plural, the singular antecedent should come first, and the pronoun should agree with the plural antecedent (*Neither Johnson nor his sons know **their** business*).

The following words are singular, and when they are the antecedent of a pronoun, the pronoun should also be singular:

    anybody   each   everybody   somebody   no one
    anyone   every   everyone   nobody   someone

These words also take a singular verb, of course, if they are the subject of a sentence:

    Nobody is eager to risk **his** life.
    Everybody does **his** work efficiently.
    We have selected each of the men on the basis of **his** merit.

When the sex of the antecedent is unknown, as in words such as *everyone,* the pronoun is masculine (*Everyone in the class did **his** homework*).

A. Fill in the missing elements in the following chart.

	Singular	*Plural*	*Singular Possessive*	*Plural Possessive*
First Person	I		my	
	me			
Second Person			your	
Third Person		they		their

pronouns (1)

UNIT 5

pronouns (2)

When to Use *That* as a Relative Pronoun

That, who, whom, or *which* are used in dependent clauses. In some sentences, *that* is preferred to the other relative pronouns. If leaving out the clause that follows a relative pronoun would drastically change the meaning of the sentence, select *that* rather than *who, whom,* or *which.* Most people have no trouble selecting the right word when they speak, but because *who, whom,* or *which* seem more formal, using them in sentences where *that* is the correct choice is a fairly common error in written material.

> A man **that** I knew was at the party.   Juan, **whom** I know, was at the party.

A. Combine each pair of sentences below into one sentence with a clause that begins with a relative pronoun. Use the correct relative pronoun.

EXAMPLES: I can't find the book. I want it.
I can't find the book that I want.

He is married to Maria. Maria is very beautiful.
He is married to Maria, who is very beautiful.

1. I ate the cake. My mother baked it.

2. I hope you will like the cake. It is lemon with chocolate frosting.

3. I saw the cat. The cat is frightening the birds on our bird feeder.

4. Because it was overdue at the library, I returned the book. It was about Africa.

B. In each sentence, underline the correct relative pronoun in parentheses.

1. The book (that, which) I read was an interesting one.
2. The dog, (that, which) was black and white, was chasing the cat.
3. They never found the treasure (that, which) they were looking for.
4. The man (that, whom) we want is aggressive, hard-working, and personable.
5. The executive office, (that, which) is in Chicago, is too far from the plant.

If the relative pronoun can be left out without destroying the sentence (*The woman (that) I met was young*), select the relative pronoun *that*.

Pronouns and Their Antecedents

When locating the antecedent, disregard a phrase beginning with *as well as, in addition to,* or *and not* (*John, and not his brothers, is on **his** way*).

A. Write the correct pronoun in the blank in each sentence.

EXAMPLE: Jack and Jill are on ___their___ way.

1. The Acme Company and the Ajax Company are merging _____ assets.
2. Either Miss Smith or Miss Black will get _____ wish.
3. Neither the boys nor the girls are ready for _____ lessons.
4. Neither the teacher nor the people in his class were ready for _____ test.
5. Each of our competitors has reduced _____ sales.
6. Each of the factories is operating at _____ fullest capacity.
7. Not a person left _____ seat before the last curtain.
8. One of the students left _____ books.
9. The boys, in addition to John, are on _____ way.
10. John, as well as his brothers, is on _____ way.

Words like *committee, jury, class, crowd,* and *army* may be singular or plural depending on the meaning of the sentence. When referred to as a single unit, a word like this is singular (*The army went **its** way*); when referring to the individuals that make up the group, it is plural (*The committee were called at **their** homes*).

B. Write the correct pronoun in the blank in each sentence.

1. The committee is holding _____ meeting.
2. The class is in _____ room.
3. The jury brought in _____ split verdict.
4. The manager expects every man to do _____ best.
5. Our firm expects all its employees to do _____ best.

UNIT 5

pronouns (3)

The Antecedents and Numbers of Pronouns

You have already learned to recognize the relative pronouns *who, which,* and *that.* These pronouns are often followed by a verb that must agree in number with the antecedent of these relative pronouns. You must use reasoning to decide which antecedent belongs to them.

> She is one of those girls who **are** conscientious in following directions.
> She is the only girl of all the applicants who **is** able to do the job.

Reasoning tells you that in the first sentence, the antecedent of *who* is *girls,* plural, and that in the second, it is *girl,* singular.

A. In the column marked "Pronoun," write the pronoun. In the column marked "Antecedent," write the antecedent. In the column marked "Number," write *S* if the antecedent is singular, write *P* if the antecedent is plural.

	Pronoun	*Antecedent*	*Number*
EXAMPLE: The man appalled the doctor by his condition.	his	man	S
1. The present equipment deserves all the praise given it.			
2. Mr. Jones is certain of his grounds.			
3. The Acme Laundry knows it can count on continued community support.			
4. The boy's rackets were hung on their sides.			
5. Mr. Jones can protect the firm if he acts quickly.			
6. Our firm is proud of its record.			

7. Somebody forgot his glasses. _____ _____ _____

8. Each of the players has his part. _____ _____ _____

9. Mr. Jones and Mr. Smith are on their way to
   the meeting. _____ _____ _____

10. Mr. Jones, as well as Mr. Smith, is on his way
    to the meeting. _____ _____ _____

11. Each man must do his very best. _____ _____ _____

12. The committee has been in its meeting room
    for hours. _____ _____ _____

13. Neither the desk nor the table is worth its price. _____ _____ _____

14. Mr. Roberts, in addition to the entire staff,
    will offer his resignation. _____ _____ _____

15. Neither Mrs. Jones nor the boys have saved
    their money. _____ _____ _____

Clarity in Using Pronouns

When using pronouns in your writing, be sure that the antecedent of the pronoun is clearly understood.

> The manager told Brown that the meaning of **his** report was unclear.

The sentence does not make clear whose report is involved—Brown's or the manager's. In such a case, it is better to reword the sentence:

> The manager told Brown that the meaning of Brown's report was unclear.

A. In the space provided, write the correct pronoun.

1. Smith and Jones has grown till (it, they) is the largest firm in (its, it's, their) field.
   _____

2. If somebody does an outstanding job, (he, they) will be rewarded for (his, their) efforts.
   _____

3. The memoranda (is, are) in (its, their) proper place. _____

4. Every girl in that class knows (his, her, their) lessons. _____

5. The crisis (is, are) over but has left (its, their) mark. _____

6. Now is the time for all good men to come to the aid of (his, their) country. _____

7. Each good man should come to the aid of (his, their) country. _____

8. No one in this world is certain of (his, their) future; yet each must plan as best

   (he, they) can. _____

Page 44   pronouns (3)

UNIT 5

pronouns (4)

Finding the Antecedent of Relative Pronouns

A. In each sentence, draw two lines under the relative pronoun. Draw one line under its antecedent.

EXAMPLE: This is the machine that I want repaired.

1. I saw the worker who repaired the typewriter.
2. Is he the man who sent you here?
3. There are many mothers who are now in the labor force in the U.S.A.
4. Those who analyze their finances sometimes find they are adding little to the family's income.
5. It is the rare woman who earns as much as her husband.
6. Even when the work that she performs is the same as that performed by men, she often receives less pay.
7. She often has to pay for child care, which is not always of the best.
8. The women whom we are discussing are often dismayed to find how large their income taxes are.
9. One answer to the problem that faces mothers may be part-time work.
10. There are several firms that are engaged in providing this kind of work.
11. Paid public-service positions is the solution that some women have found.
12. The men who fill these positions often have full-time jobs elsewhere.
13. The woman to whom it is an only job may be more successful than such a man.
14. A working mother who is careful will make sure that the medical benefits of her job do not duplicate her husband's.
15. If she has an employer who is withdrawing too little income tax, she should put extra money in the bank to be prepared for April 15.

Possessive Pronouns

A. In the space provided, write the proper word. Remember that you do not add apostrophes to possessive pronouns.

1. The book fell on (its) (it's) side. _____
2. (Its) (It's) going to be a cold winter. _____
3. The package on top is (ours) (our's). _____
4. They claimed the package was (theirs) (there's) (their's). _____
5. These men are certain (their) (they're) correct. _____
6. Mr. Jones is a man (who) (that) can get his own way. _____
7. Victory is (our's) (ours). _____
8. The pact must stand or fall on (its) (it's) merits. _____
9. (Yours) (Your's) truly, _____
10. Here is the man (that) (which) I told you about. _____
11. This car of (ours) (our's) is similar to (yours) (your's) (yours'). _____
12. This work of (hers) (her's) is extremely clear in (its) (it's) analysis of (there) (their) accounting department. _____
13. (Its) (It's) not clear whether the package is (yours) (your's) or (theirs) (their's) (theres) (there's). _____
14. Tell me (whose) (who's) letter is more accurate, mine or (hers) (her's). _____
15. The company hurt (its) (it's) reputation, (its) (it's) sad to say. _____

Practice pronouncing all of the syllables in *accidentally*, *naturally*, and other words that end in *-ally*. If you say and hear the *-al-*, you will remember not to leave it out when you spell the words.

Page 46   pronouns (4)

UNIT 5
pronouns (5)

A. In each sentence, underline the correct form of the word in parentheses.

1. We'll go as soon as (your, you're) ready.
2. An animal that is hunted is unlikely to think of mankind as (it's, its) friend.
3. The metropolitan area is struggling to find an answer to (it's, its) problems.
4. The supermarket (that, which) you need is reliable and economical.
5. The firm is proud of (it's, its) history.

B. Write the correct form of the word in the space provided.

1. Acme Lumber, in addition to Zenith Lumber, is launching (its, their) annual campaign.

2. The President, but not his Cabinet, is on (his, their) way. _____

3. All the members (has, have) received (his, their) invitations. _____

4. Each of the books (has, have) been autographed on (its, their) cover. _____

5. This is one of those problems that (is, are) not easily solved on (its, their) bare facts.

6. Neither Mary nor Madeline (was, were) able to do (his, her, their) special report on time. _____

7. None of the manufacturers (is, are) willing to make (his, their) contribution yet. _____

8. Mr. James, accompanied by his sons, (was, were) able to make (his, their) entrance at the appropriate moment. _____

9. He is one of those men who (is, are) always complaining about (his, their) tasks.

10. He is different from any of those executives who (remain, remains) calm when (he, they) (is, are) harassed. _____

Page 47

Do not feel that using a dictionary to find the correct spelling of a word is a confession of ignorance. English spelling is so irregular that even professional writers use a dictionary often to check on spelling.

Review

A. Possessive pronouns are spelled incorrectly in the following letter. Rewrite the letter using them correctly.

Dear Mr. Byrnes:

    Thank you for your order of a years supply of Danity Perfumes which your buyer, Mr. Stoll, gave us yesterday.

    Your's is an unusually large order and this, combined with Mr. Stolls extreme courtesy, is appreciated. Our's is a small firm, and an order the size of yours is very encouraging.

    We know that our line of perfumes will meet the perfume needs of a number of your departments.

    You will find Danity Perfume's are an especially good item for your Womens Toiletry Department. In addition, it's success has been proven in the Debs Department of many stores.

    If we can be of any further service, please call upon us.

                                          Very truly yours',

UNIT 5

pronouns (6)

assignment

A. The following letter contains a number of errors, particularly in the use of pronouns. Cross out each incorrectly spelled word and write the correct form above it.

Dear Miss Johnson:

We were extremely pleased to be invited by P.C.L. to attend it's annual convention. I know that each of the members of our staff felt it their personal duty and pleasure to attend. Mr. Smith, as well as Mr. Johnson, send their special thanks to you for the invitation.

I was especially thrilled by the talks given by Professor Poole and Dean Brown. Their's is an unusual combination of talents. I noticed that during there talks every member of the audience were glued to their seats. Its a rarity in this day and age to meet men who have such complete command of his English and his subject matter.

I also wish to congratulate you on the fine job done by your banquet committee. Every table decoration, every knife, every fork were in their proper places. The banquet speakers, especially Miss Green, did her work exceptionally well. By the way, Miss Green is the woman which I told you about at lunch last week. I'm very much pleased that talent such as her's was recognized by your committee. She is one of those women who is reliable and can be trusted to do her work to it's fullest extent. Neither Mr. Smith nor Mr. Johnson were disappointed in their expectations.

In closing, let me say that I believe wholeheartedly in the work of this organization of your's. Since ours' is a small firm, we are especially proud to be members. You will probably be pleased to know that neither Mr. Smith nor any of his associates has had a word of criticism of your organization.

Sincerely,

A. Write the correct form of the pronoun at the end of each sentence.

1. England expects every man this day to do (his, their) duty. _____

2. Each student should bring (his, their) dictionary to class. _____

3. (They're, their) planning to arrive at seven. _____

4. Each of the club members waited for (his, their) turn. _____

5. Glendenning and Smith, Inc., is having (its, it's, their) account audited. _____

6. Every piece of paper, every eraser, every pencil has (its, their) place on her desk.

_____

7. The crowd let (its, their) anger be known. _____

8. The people (who, that) I know best are in the advertising business. _____

9. His statement was not quite so strongly worded as (hers, her's). _____

10. My coat is more fashionable than (yours, your's). _____

11. Every member of all the platoons should present (his, their) arms for inspection. _____

12. All orders should be identified by (its, their) own number. _____

13. The problems of the production department would be less if (they, it) had more money.

_____

14. The house (which, that) I liked best was white. _____

15. The company's policies (which, that) are paternalistic have been in effect for a long time.

_____

In general, adjectives of one or two syllables form the comparative and superlative by adding *-er* and *-est* (*prettier, prettiest*); adjectives of three or more syllables form the comparative and superlative with the words *more* and *most* (*more beautiful, most beautiful*).

UNIT 6

verb types and tenses (1)

Introduction

Most verbs can be classified as either *action verbs* or *linking verbs*. Here are simple examples of how action and linking verbs differ:

>The car **swerved** off the road.   It **seems** a good idea.

Another name for *linking verbs* is *state-of-being* verbs. Whereas action verbs tell what happens or happened, linking verbs simply tell what is or what was. Some words like *taste* in the following examples can be either action or linking verbs.

>The gourmet **tasted** the soup with delight.   Candy **tastes** sweet.

In the first sentence, an action takes place. In the second, no action takes place. If *is,* or some form of it, can be substituted for a verb, it is a linking verb (Candy **is** sweet).

Since understanding the distinction between action and linking verbs is important in later units, be sure you recognize all the forms that can be made from the verb *be* (*is, was, am,* and so forth), and remember that whenever they can be substituted for a verb in a sentence, that verb is a linking verb.

Verbs change form according to the time of the event they depict. We call the different forms verbs may take *tenses*. Except for verbs with irregular forms, which are covered in the following unit, few people have trouble using the correct tense when they speak. Since sentences are often more complicated in written English, however, it is worth your while to learn the name and use of each tense. Using verbs skillfully and confidently is an important skill in business writing.

The following chart shows the tenses, and uses the word *walk* as an example. If you can cover the examples, and say the correct forms, you already know the names of the tenses. If not, study the chart before going on to learn the meaning of the various tenses.

Active

	Simple	Progressive
Present	I walk	I am walking
Past	I walked	I was walking
Future	I will walk	I will be walking
Present Perfect	I have walked	I have been walking
Past Perfect	I had walked	I had been walking
Future Perfect	I will have walked	I will have been walking

Though not all verbs can be used in the passive, *walk* occasionally is, so we will continue to use it as our example of the tenses in the passive voice.

Passive

	Simple	Progressive
Present	I am walked	I am being walked
Past	I was walked	I was being walked
Future	I will be walked	I will be being walked
Present Perfect	I have been walked	I have been being walked
Past Perfect	I had been walked	I had been being walked
Future Perfect	I will have been walked	I will have been being walked

If your native language is a European one other than English, note how many more words are used in English than in your native language to express the meanings of most of the tenses. Because the endings of the verb are few, other words must be used before the verb, and their order is important. Make sure you pronounce these small words correctly in order to make yourself easily understood, and make sure you use them in the right order.

Action and Linking Verbs

A. After each sentence, write the predicate verb (the verb that goes with the subject). In the next column, write *A* if it is an action verb. Write *L* if it is a linking verb.

	Predicate Verb	Action or Linking
1. This booklet will show our entire line of clothing.		
2. We feel certain of your success.		
3. Did you feel the texture of the cloth?		
4. The meal tasted wonderful.		
5. I tasted the soup.		

UNIT 6
verb types and tenses (2)

The Simple Tenses

No matter what the person (*I, you, he, we, they*), with one exception, the verb ending remains the same in all tenses. That exception is the third person singular. If the subject of a verb is a noun or *he, she,* or *it,* the verb takes an *-s* on the end. *I walk, he walks.*

If you come from a part of the country where this *-s* is sometimes dropped in pronunciation, practice saying verbs, pronouncing the *-s* clearly.

The past tense refers to a definite past action or event.

> I went to the movies yesterday.
> I sold the books last year.

The future tense applies to events that will take place at a future time, and is formed by placing *will* (sometimes *shall*) before the verb. Today, most people use only the form *will,* but traditionalists still require these forms:

> I shall walk   we shall walk
> you will walk   you will walk
> he will walk   they will walk

To express determination or emotion, the traditional way was to transpose the *shalls* and *wills* in the above chart. *He shall go* meant *He must go. Should* and *would* were used similarly: *I should like to see you,* but *He said you would like to see me.* Today, however, at least in the United States, this is no longer considered the only correct usage by most authorities. *Will* can be used to form the future tense for all persons. *Should* remains fairly common in the expression *I should like,* but otherwise *I would* is more common.

Page 53

A. After each verb, write the pronoun in parentheses and the simple present, past, and future forms that agree with the pronoun.

EXAMPLE:	*Present*	*Past*	*Future*
(she) wait	she waits	she waited	she will wait
1. (I) work			
2. (they) dine			
3. (he) pick			
4. (it) receive			
5. (we) last			
6. (you) eradicate			
7. (I) fold			
8. (we) rule			
9. (it) emit			
10. (it) occur			
11. (I) concede			
12. (it) recede			
13. (they) follow			
14. (she) allow			
15. (it) seem			

The final *-r* in *prefer* and *refer* is not doubled when *-ence* is added because the accent is on the first syllable in *preference* and *reference*. In *referred* and *preferred* the accent is on the last syllable of the root word, so the final consonant is doubled.

The Progressive Form

The progressive form is used to refer to an unfinished action.

> I am working on the books right now.
> I was studying when John came in.

When *-ing* is added to a verb, the word is called a present participle. (A past participle ends in *-ed*.) When a verb is in the form of a present participle, it takes a form of the word *be* before the participle.

UNIT 6

verb types and tenses (3)

The Perfect Tenses

In the term *perfect tense*, the word *perfect* means completed, just as the *progressive* in the *progressive tense* means *progressing* or *still going on*.

> I had shipped the order by the time the message arrived.

The form of the verb that is used in all perfect tenses is called the *perfect participle*. For example, *brought* is the perfect participle of the verb *bring*.

There are three perfect tenses:

Present Perfect:	has (have) brought
Past Perfect:	had brought
Future Perfect:	shall (or will) have brought

Use the present perfect tense to refer to an action that was completed in the past but is part of a series of actions that continues into the present. The sign of the present perfect is the word *has* or *have* before the verb.

> He **has** shopped in our store many times.

The past perfect tense shows action that was completed before another event in the past occurred. The sign of the past perfect is the word *had* before the verb.

> I **had** shipped the order **by the time** the message arrived.

Use the future perfect tense to show action that will be completed by a definite time in the future. Use *shall have* or *will have* before the verb.

A. In each sentence, ask yourself: "Was the event completed before the other took place?" Decide on the proper form of the verb and write it after each sentence.

EXAMPLES: It (stop) raining by noon.   _____had stopped_____

John (file) only one report so far.   _____has filed_____

1. They (hide) the prizes before the party began. _____
2. He (finish) college before the war was over. _____
3. We (print) the edition before the censorship order arrived. _____
4. We (suspect) his statement even before we received the police report. _____
5. Spring (arrive) early last year. _____
6. By the time the message arrives, John (left). _____
7. The Smiths (travel) to this park year after year. _____
8. Since you left this office, there (be) very little activity. _____
9. I (be) in this office since 9 A.M. _____
10. The clerk (stay) on the job since 1942. _____
11. The printer (proofread) this paper before he left last night. _____
12. I (work) on this job since graduating. _____
13. The mail (arrive) before we opened the office. _____
14. Our department (ship) the order before we received your wire. _____
15. We (see) him walking in the street yesterday. _____

Review

A. Write the correct form of the word in the space provided.

1. The committee is holding (its, their) meeting. _____
2. John, accompanied by his brothers, did (his, their) best. _____
3. The dog hurt (its, it's) tail. _____
4. England expects every man to do (their, his) duty. _____
5. The car (that, which) you have is an antique. _____
6. They will come when (you're, your) through with your work. _____
7. Which one is (you're, your) book? _____
8. The child (that, whom) we will visit is six years old. _____
9. Neither Helen nor Joan has read (her, their) book. _____
10. (Whose, Who's) phone number are you dialing? _____

name section date

UNIT 6

verb types and tenses (4)

assignment

A. In the space next to each verb mark *A* if it is an action verb; mark *L* if it is a linking verb; mark *E* if it could be either.

1. explode _____
2. spend _____
3. had been _____
4. sleep _____
5. lie _____
6. were _____
7. seem _____
8. walk _____
9. would have been _____
10. looks _____
11. was _____
12. recline _____
13. rested _____
14. mail _____
15. becoming _____
16. thinks _____
17. tastes _____
18. attack _____
19. receives _____
20. feels _____
21. taste _____
22. smell _____
23. touch _____
24. appear _____
25. desire _____
26. break _____
27. fall _____
28. will be _____
29. drive _____
30. looked _____

The purpose of the final *e* in *shine* is to indicate that the *i* is long. Any vowel following a single consonant preceded by a single vowel usually has this effect. This is the reason for dropping the final *e* in such words before adding a suffix beginning with a vowel.

Words that end in -v are rare. Even though the preceding vowel is short in *love* and *glove,* the -e appears at the end to avoid having the word ending in -v.

B. Using each perfect participle, write the present perfect, past perfect, and future perfect tenses.

EXAMPLE:	*Present Perfect*	*Past Perfect*	*Future Perfect*
print	has (or have) printed	had printed	shall (or will) have printed
1. shipped			
2. left			
3. sat			
4. taken			
5. raised			

C. After each sentence, write the proper tense of the verb.

EXAMPLE: John (read) when the telephone rang.   was reading

1. Mrs. Smith (bake) a cake yesterday afternoon. _____
2. Susan (go) to Europe next summer. _____
3. He (drive) to the store for milk right now. _____
4. I (be) glad you are here now. _____
5. He (visit) the doctor's office last week. _____
6. We (suspect) him even before we received the report. _____
7. He shall (leave) by the time your plane lands. _____
8. We (talk) to him every day last week. _____
9. He (sell) his motorcycle last month. _____
10. She (sew) when you arrived. _____

UNIT 7

regular and irregular verbs (1)

Introduction

Most verbs are what we call *regular* verbs. They form the past tense by adding *-d* or *-ed* to the present tense and they form the present perfect tense by placing *has* or *have* before the past tense.

The following chart shows some regular verbs:

Present	Past	Present Perfect
receive	received	has or have received
like	liked	has or have liked
follow	followed	has or have followed

There are many verbs which do not form their past and perfect tenses in this manner. They are called *irregular* verbs. We can arrange most of the irregular verbs into six groups with similar sound patterns. If you read aloud the verbs in each pattern group you should master these irregular verbs easily. As you repeat the words in each group let your mind hear the pattern.

1.
Present	Past	Perfect
bring	brought	has brought
buy	bought	has bought
fight	fought	has fought
seek	sought	has sought
teach	taught	has taught

2.
Present	Past	Perfect
begin	began	has begun
swim	swam	has swum
ring	rang	has rung
sing	sang	has sung
spring	sprang	has sprung
sink	sank	has sunk
shrink	shrank	has shrunk
drink	drank	has drunk
run	ran	has run

3.
Present	Past	Perfect
blow	blew	has blown
grow	grew	has grown
know	knew	has known
throw	threw	has thrown
fly	flew	has flown
draw	drew	has drawn
withdraw	withdrew	has withdrawn
wear	wore	has worn
swear	swore	has sworn
tear	tore	has torn
show	showed	has shown

4.
Present	Past	Perfect
bend	bent	has bent
lend	lent	has lent
spend	spent	has spent

Page 59

Present	Past	Perfect
deal	dealt	has dealt
feel	felt	has felt
keep	kept	has kept
sleep	slept	has slept
sweep	swept	has swept
weep	wept	has wept
mean	meant	has meant
leave	left	has left
lose	lost	has lost

5.
Present	Past	Perfect
break	broke	has broken
choose	chose	has chosen
freeze	froze	has frozen
speak	spoke	has spoken
steal	stole	has stolen
forget	forgot	has forgotten

6.
Present	Past	Perfect
strive	strove	has striven
arise	arose	has arisen
take	took	has taken
mistake	mistook	has mistaken
shake	shook	has shaken
write	wrote	has written
typewrite	typewrote	has typewritten
underwrite	underwrote	has underwritten
eat	ate	has eaten
fall	fell	has fallen
forbid	forbade	has forbidden
give	gave	has given
hide	hid	has hidden

Some verbs are irregular because they are the same in the present, past, and perfect tenses.

Present	Past	Perfect
bid	bid	has bid
burst	burst	has burst
cost	cost	has cost
cut	cut	has cut
forecast	forecast	has forecast

Present	Past	Perfect
hurt	hurt	has hurt
let	let	has let
put	put	has put
quit	quit	has quit
spread	spread	has spread
thrust	thrust	has thrust

The following irregular verbs follow no particular pattern. You will have to review the list until you can repeat each form of the verb automatically.

Present	Past	Perfect
come	came	has come
become	became	has become
bleed	bled	has bled
lead	led	has led
flee	fled	has fled
get	got	has got
meet	met	has met
bind	bound	has bound
stand	stood	has stood

Present	Past	Perfect
win	won	has won
hold	held	has held
stick	stuck	has stuck
strike	struck	has struck
string	strung	has strung
have	had	has had
say	said	has said
make	made	has made
do	did	has done
go	went	has gone

UNIT 7

regular and irregular verbs (2)

Irregular Verbs

A. On each line the present tense of an irregular verb is printed. Write the past tense and the past perfect tense of each of these verbs.

Present	Past	Past Perfect
EXAMPLE:		
I fly	I _____flew_____	I _____had flown_____
1. I am	I _____	I _____
2. You blow	You _____	You _____
3. It breaks	It _____	It _____
4. It bursts	It _____	It _____
5. They cost	They _____	They _____
6. You deal	You _____	You _____
7. We drive	We _____	We _____
8. I forbid	I _____	I _____
9. We forecast	We _____	We _____
10. They do	They _____	They _____
11. I hide	I _____	I _____
12. She knows	She _____	She _____
13. I lead	I _____	I _____
14. You mistake	You _____	You _____
15. We pay	We _____	We _____

It is easier and quicker to use a dictionary that you are familiar with. Get your own paperback dictionary and carry it with your other books.

B. In the space provided, write the correct form of the irregular verb for each sentence.

EXAMPLE: He has (lose) his opportunity.   lost

1. I (awake) at the crack of dawn yesterday.   _____
2. By the time he arrived, she had (become) very tired.   _____
3. The general had (awake) by the time I called.   _____
4. I (bid) $50 for the vase at yesterday's auction.   _____
5. They were (bind) to each other by a common interest.   _____
6. The tire had (blow) out.   _____
7. Her heart had been (break) by the cad.   _____
8. We will (build) a factory on the river.   _____
9. Yesterday the pipe (burst) with a roar.   _____
10. He was (choose) to accompany you.   _____
11. He has (come) a long way.   _____
12. By noon it had already (cost) me my entire salary.   _____
13. It was (cut) across the top.   _____
14. They were (deal) with in short order.   _____
15. He has (do) no wrong.   _____

The reasons for most of our irregular spellings are historical. In the Middle Ages, *u* was written *v*. When the vowel sound in *word* was spelled as it was pronounced, as "u," the word *word* was written "wvrd." Medieval scribes didn't think this "looked right"—hence when the sound usually spelled *u* comes after *w*, it is spelled *o*.

Page 62   regular and irregular verbs (2)

name　　　　　　　　　　　　section　　　　　　　　　　　　date

UNIT 7

regular and irregular verbs (3)

Irregular Verbs

A. On each line the present tense of an irregular verb is printed. Write the past tense and the present perfect tense of each of these verbs.

Present	*Past*	*Present Perfect*
EXAMPLE: I begin	I _____ began _____	I _____ have begun _____
1. He reads	He _____	He _____
2. You seek	You _____	You _____
3. I shrink	I _____	I _____
4. We sing	We _____	We _____
5. You speak	You _____	You _____
6. I spend	I _____	I _____
7. They stand	They _____	They _____
8. We take	We _____	We _____
9. She teaches	She _____	She _____
10. We tear	We _____	We _____
11. You throw	You _____	You _____
12. I typewrite	I _____	I _____
13. He wears	He _____	He _____
14. I withdraw	I _____	I _____
15. You write	You _____	You _____

Nonstandard forms of English often have advantages that standard English does not have. *I be sick* **and** *I am sick* **have different meanings in one kind of nonstandard English. The former means** *I am sick much of the time;* **the latter,** *I am sick now.* **In standard English the verb form does not make this distinction, since only** *I am sick* **is correct.**

B. In the space provided, write the correct form of the irregular verb for each sentence.

1. This convention has (draw) a huge crowd. _____
2. He had (drink) too much water. _____
3. We discovered that prices had (fall). _____
4. Father (forbid) their leaving the house. _____
5. Planes have (fly) millions of miles. _____
6. The weather department has (forecast) clearing skies. _____
7. By morning the water had (freeze). _____
8. He has (get) too big for his breeches. _____
9. The prize was (give) to the bookkeeper. _____
10. All the members had (go) before the bell sounded. _____
11. Our nation has (grow) to enormous power. _____
12. He has not (hear) of your product. _____
13. The invoice was (hide) under a pile of paper. _____
14. He had (hurt) himself. _____
15. Have you (keep) up with the news? _____
16. He (go) to Chicago to attend the convention. _____
17. He (stand) before the members and spoke at length. _____
18. The book was (bind) in leather. _____
19. I was (strike) by the beauty of the sunset. _____
20. The bubble of inflation had (burst). _____

Page 64   regular and irregular verbs (3)

UNIT 7

regular and irregular verbs (4)

Irregular Verbs

A. In the space provided, write the correct form of the irregular verb for each sentence.

1. He had (meet) most of them before. _____
2. I had (mistake) you for him. _____
3. Your account was (overdraw). _____
4. He has (prepay) the postage. _____
5. Have you (read) the contract? _____
6. We had (put) the matter before the board. _____
7. Had he (quit) the race by the end of the first mile? _____
8. The race had been (run) before noon. _____
9. He had (see) many examples, but could follow none. _____
10. They have (seek) the answer in vain. _____
11. The building had (shake) under the force of the earthquake. _____
12. Had he (show) you how to operate it? _____
13. The profits (shrink) last week to half their former level. _____
14. She has (sing) the song before royalty. _____
15. The ship had (sink) to the bottom. _____

The past participles of many verbs are also used as adjectives: an *overdrawn* account, *prepaid* postage.

Review

A. After each verb, write the pronoun in parentheses and the simple present, past, and future forms that agree with the pronoun.

	Present	*Past*	*Future*
EXAMPLE: (he) walk	he walks	he walked	he will walk
1. (they) like			
2. (I) type			
3. (you) turn			
4. (we) paint			
5. (he) brush			

B. After each verb, write the pronoun in parentheses and the present perfect, past perfect, and future perfect forms that agree with the pronoun.

	Present Perfect	*Past Perfect*	*Future Perfect*
EXAMPLE: (I) allow	I have allowed	I had allowed	I shall (or will) have allowed
1. (we) travel			
2. (you) shop			
3. (it) bark			
4. (they) listen			
5. (she) watch			

C. In each sentence, underline the correct form of the verb in parentheses.

EXAMPLE: He (sees, <u>is seeing</u>) the dentist now.

1. She (read, was reading) when her friend arrived.
2. Mrs. Hogan (typed, was typing) the letter earlier today.
3. John (ran, was running) when he tripped and fell down.
4. We (worked, were working) hard last week.
5. They (rode, were riding) their bicycles every day last week.

name　　　　　　　　　　　　　　section　　　　　　　　　　　　　　date

UNIT 7

regular and irregular verbs (5)

assignment

The first half of a letter appears on this page, and the concluding half on page 68. The letter contains a number of regular and irregular verbs. Above each verb in parentheses write the correct form of the verb as it is used in each sentence. Be sure to read each sentence through carefully before you write your answer.

Dear Mr. Robinson:

　　I (be) very disappointed that you (do) not send your representative to watch the test of our new Starfire car model last week. We are positive that he would have (be) astounded by the way the Starfire (perform), as (be) the hundreds of others who (be) there. Did he (forget) the date of this demonstration test?

　　If he had (attend), he would (see) a new concept in automotive design and engineering. The Starfire (be) an all-new car. It (have) a new engine, new streamlining, new controls.

　　Until the new line of Starfires was (unveil) last week, the automobile industry (have) been lagging behind other industries in the use of plastics. The Starfire (have) changed this.

　　At last week's demonstration tests, the Starfire (accelerate) to 90 miles per hour in under 25 seconds.

　　I needn't tell you how (astonish) the representatives of other firms (be) when they (see) this spectacular performance. I'm sure that many of them had already told you about it themselves.

Page 67

The following is the continuation of the letter begun on page 67. Above each verb in parentheses write the correct form of the verb as it is used in each sentence.

    Until you have (see) the Starfire and have (ride) in it, you will be missing the thrill of your life. If I (be) you, I would make arrangements to attend the next demonstration, which will be (hold) next Thursday at four o'clock at the Grand Plaza Arena. We know that by six o'clock next Thursday you will be convinced that your going to the demonstration (be) one of the wisest moves of your life.

    Moreover, I am pleased to (inform) you that your firm (have) been chosen to enjoy a particular distinction at next week's demonstration. I am (forbid) to disclose anything further, but I can forecast with certainty that you will be (freeze) with surprise.

    You have (know) our firm for many years. You have (see) us become the leader in our field. You know that during the past three years we have (spend) many millions of dollars to build the Starfire and that we will spend many millions more to improve it. We have (strive) to shake off the shackles of conservative thinking that have (hold) the automotive industry back for years. We have (undertake) a difficult task these past three years. While others were sitting in their easy chairs, our research men were striving for perfection.

    The Starfire has been (bring) into being by this devotion to a concept. It has (spring) into being out of the minds and energy of America's top automotive engineers. In the same way that the jet plane (shrink) the highways of the air, so shall the Starfire shrink the highways on land.

    Won't you find out for yourself all about the Starfire?

                                           Sincerely,

UNIT 8
more about verbs (1)

Introduction

There are three types of words which are derived from verbs. These types of words, called **verbals,** are *infinitives, participles,* and *gerunds.*

Infinitives: The first verbal we will discuss is the *infinitive.* An infinitive is simply a verb with the word *to* in front of it: *to love, to have loved; to see, to have been seen.*

Here is an example of an infinitive used in a sentence:

I wish **to visit** you frequently.

You have probably heard the expression *to split an infinitive.* This means that a word has been placed between *to* and the verb. This "splitting" is generally not considered good English because it produces an unclear and awkward-sounding sentence.

I have **to** sadly **leave** you.

Good usage requires:

Sadly, I have **to leave** you.

Participles: The second verbal we will discuss is the *participle.* In Unit 6 you learned that when you add *ing* to the verb you have what is called a *present participle* and that the present participle can be used as the *progressive* form of the verb.

However, sometimes this same present participle is used in a phrase which describes the subject of the sentence:

Working steadily, John finished his job by noon.

The participial phrase *working steadily* describes the subject, *John.*
When a participial phrase begins a sentence, the subject must be stated clearly *immediately* after the phrase. When the subject of a sentence is not stated immediately after the phrase we say that the participle is *dangling.* Sentences which have dangling participles can be most peculiar in meaning. Here is an example:

Climbing the trees and swinging in the branches, the old lady noticed **the monkeys.**

Since the climbing and swinging were done by the monkeys, the sentence should read:

>Climbing the trees and swinging in the branches, **the monkeys** were noticed by the old lady.

Gerunds: The third verbal is the *gerund*. A gerund is a verb with an *ing* ending which is used as a noun. Look at this sentence:

>I like **swimming.**

You could substitute *baseball* or any other noun for the word *swimming*. Here is a sentence using the gerund *jogging*:

>**Jogging** is good for your health.

Parallel Construction

In writing and speaking English it is important to keep in mind the idea of *parallel construction*. Look at the two sentences below.

>I like **swimming, boating,** and **to hike.**
>I like **swimming, boating,** and **hiking.**

In the first sentence we are using two gerunds (*swimming* and *boating*) and one infinitive (*to hike*). In the second sentence we are using three gerunds. The second sentence is constructed in a parallel manner.

To keep the sentence construction parallel you should use the same type of verbal throughout. Either use all gerunds or all infinitives, as in these examples:

>I like **reading, painting,** and **playing** the piano.
>I like **to read, to paint,** and **to play** the piano.

Transitive and Intransitive Verbs: You know that a sentence must contain a noun or a pronoun as its subject and a verb as its predicate. Sometimes you can combine a noun and a verb and still not have a meaningful sentence:

>The secretary mailed.

What we need is an object of the verb *mailed*, a word that will tell us what was mailed. In this sentence *letter* is the object:

>The secretary mailed the **letter.**

To find the object of a verb ask yourself whom or what after the verb.

Many verbs do not require objects to complete the meaning of a sentence. Note this example:

>The President speaks.

A verb that needs an object to make sense is called a *transitive verb*, since the action transfers to the object. A verb that does not need an object is called an *intransitive verb*. Its action is complete in itself.

UNIT 8
more about verbs (2)

Verbals and Parallel Construction

A. Some of the sentences below are not constructed in a parallel manner. Rewrite these sentences. If the sentence is correct, write *C* on the line.

EXAMPLE: On a vacation we should plan to rest, traveling, and to exercise.
           On a vacation we should plan resting, traveling, and exercising.

    OR: On a vacation we should plan to rest, to travel, and to exercise.

1. Reading broadens a person, writing sharpens him, and conversing stimulates him.

2. Speaking, listening, and to take notes are student activities.

3. He likes to swim, to play ball, and boating.

4. Sewing and to play tennis are her favorite pastimes.

Transitive and Intransitive Verbs

A. Each of the following sentences contains a verb and its object. In the space provided, rewrite the verb and the object of that verb.

	Verb	Object of Verb
EXAMPLE: Mr. Smith sent me to the factory.	sent	me
1. Our firm makes the finest clothing.		

Page 71

2. We hear the important events of the day on the radio. _____ _____
3. Will you mail your money by return post? _____ _____
4. They advised him against the contract. _____ _____

To lie never needs an object to complete its meaning; it is intransitive. *To lay* always needs an object; it is transitive. Here are three sentences using *to lie*. Notice that there is no object after the verb.

> I **lie** on the grass.
> I **lay** on the grass yesterday.
> I **have lain** on the grass every afternoon this week.

Here are three sentences using *to lay*. Notice the object, *book*.

> I **lay** the book on the table.
> I **laid** the book on the table yesterday.
> I **have laid** the book on the table as you asked.

B. In the space provided, write the correct form of the verb.

EXAMPLE: He has (laid, lain) in a hospital bed all week.   lain

1. The book (lay, laid) on the shelf for months. _____
2. (Lay, Lie) down before dinner. _____
3. The President (lay, laid) down our basic foreign policy. _____
4. It has (laid, lain) on a shelf for years. _____
5. He will (lie, lay) the carpet tomorrow. _____
6. Will you (lay, lie) down for a few moments' rest? _____
7. He (lay, laid) the foundations for a solid business. _____
8. They had (laid, lain) the goods on top of the table. _____
9. The goods have (laid, lain) on the table for weeks. _____
10. He had (laid, lain) his cards on the table and was ready to suffer the consequences.

UNIT 8

more about verbs (3)

Transitive and Intransitive Verbs

Here are some sentences using *to sit,* an intransitive verb.

> The director **sits** at the head of the table.
> The director **sat** at the head yesterday.
> The director **has sat** at the head at every meeting.

Here are some sentences using *to set,* a transitive verb.

> He **sets** the book on the desk.
> He **set** the book on the desk yesterday.
> He **has set** the book on the desk.

Here are some sentences using *to rise,* an intransitive verb.

> I **rise** early every morning.
> I **rose** early yesterday.
> I **have risen** early every morning this week.

Here are some sentences using *to raise,* a transitive verb.

> We **raise** the flag each morning.
> We **raised** the flag at dawn this morning.
> We **have raised** the flag every morning this summer.

Study the sentences above. Notice which verbs require objects and which do not.

A. In each sentence below, underline the correct verb in parentheses.

1. (Sit, Set) down in that chair.
2. They have (sat, set) in their rocking chairs for years.
3. Can you (raise, rise) to the situation?
4. (Set, Sit) the table down carefully.
5. Will you (raise, rise) your hand if you agree.
6. We must try to (raise, rise) above such petty bickering.
7. Can you (sit, set) by doing nothing?
8. He would have (raised, rose) prices had he foreseen the inflation.
9. Prices (raised, rose) due to the inflation.
10. (Sit, Set) the piano in the corner.

Page 73

If I Were: There is one peculiarity of the verb *to be* that you should know. It is proper for you to say *I were* and *he were* in two instances:

First, you can use these expressions to talk about a situation that you know to be *contrary to fact*.

If **I were** you, I would not talk so much.
If **he were** here, your demands would be met.

Second, it is proper to say *I were* and *he were* to express a wish:

I wish **I were** king.
I wish **he were** here now.

B. In each sentence below, underline the correct form of *to be* in parentheses.

EXAMPLE: If I (was, <u>were</u>) you, I would change my mind.

1. (Was, Were) I you, I would do the same.
2. I wish I (was, were) President.
3. He (was, were) not here yesterday.
4. If he (was, were) to disappear into thin air, I could not be more pleased.
5. I don't know if he (was, were) at the meeting.

Review

A. In the space provided, write the correct form of the irregular verb for each sentence.

EXAMPLE: He had (hurt) himself.   _____hurt_____

1. I (sleep) until noon yesterday.   _____
2. Had he (speak) to you about it?   _____
3. We (spend) many hours discussing the problem last night.   _____
4. The coil had (spring) from its covering.   _____
5. Our company has (stand) for the finest quality for 100 years.   _____
6. The two pieces had (stick) together.   _____
7. Catastrophe had (strike) the city.   _____
8. All year long he had (strive) for the top.   _____
9. He was (swear) to secrecy.   _____
10. The river had (sweep) all in its path.   _____

UNIT 8

more about verbs (4)

assignment

A. Some of the following sentences have errors concerning verbals. Rewrite the sentences correctly (you may have to add words). If the sentence is correct, write *C* on the line.

EXAMPLE: She wants to safely learn to drive.
She wants to learn to drive safely.

1. Running home, the house was seen.

2. You will like to go to the movies, to play football, and exploring.

3. He wants to read thoroughly this report.

4. Catching the ball, the point was scored by John.

5. Hearing a noise, the light went on.

B. Each of the following sentences contains a verb and its object. In the space provided, rewrite the verb and the object.

	Verb	Object of Verb
EXAMPLE: John loves Mary.	loves	Mary
1. We appreciate your letter of September 20.		

Page 75

2. We will send our representative.
3. We are enclosing a copy of the contract.
4. We discussed the entire matter with him.
5. Mrs. Jones set the book on the table.
6. The men put the lumber on the truck.
7. I laid the pencil on your desk this morning.
8. The student raised his hand knowingly.
9. She washed the dishes carefully.
10. He threw the ball to his friend.

C. In the space provided, write the correct word.

1. Have you been (sitting, setting) here all afternoon?
2. Prices had not (raised, risen) so fast as expected.
3. The journal has (laid, lain) on the shelf for years.
4. They were so tired they just (sat, set) right down on the ground.
5. The plane will (rise, raise) beyond the clouds in a few moments.
6. (Rise, Raise) the curtains and we will see better.
7. The accountant (lay, laid) the checkbook on the table.
8. Will you (lie, lay) down for a nap?
9. A number of rockets have (rose, risen) beyond the stratosphere.
10. He has (set, sat) in the same spot for hours.
11. The blame was (laid, lain) at his doorstep.
12. Will you (rise, raise) a fuss if they don't agree?
13. (Sit, Set) down at the table before the guests arrive.
14. Regulations have been (laid, lain) down by the Board.
15. Have they (sat, set) long enough to be rested?
16. Please (set, sat) the books on the table.
17. The books are (laying, lying) on the table.
18. The pilot (rose, raised) the plane to a higher altitude.
19. (Sit, Set) the hen on the eggs.
20. The United States (lie, lay) in the northern hemisphere.

UNIT 9
adjectives (1)

Introduction

An *adjective* is a word that describes or modifies a noun or pronoun. The *simple* form of an adjective describes a single item or a single group of items: *fine* book, *pretty* girls, *fast* cars, *long* letters.

Adjectives enable you to compare one item with others. If you are comparing two things, you add *-er* to most simple adjectives to make what we call the *comparative* form. Here is a sentence using the comparative form of the adjective *fast:*

Sports cars are **faster** than stock cars.

In this sentence the two items being compared are *sports cars* and *stock cars.*

Jane is **prettier** than Mary.

The adjective is *prettier; Jane* and *Mary,* two persons, are being compared.

When you compare three or more items you add *-est* to the simple adjective to make what we call the *superlative* form. Here is a sentence using the superlative form of the adjective *fast:*

This is the **fastest** sports car in the world.

One sports car is being compared with many others.

Not all adjectives form their comparatives and superlatives by adding *-er* or *-est.* Long adjectives such as *beautiful* would become tongue-twisters using that method. Instead, we place the word *more* or *most* in front of the simple adjective. Use *more* to form the comparative of long adjectives: *more beautiful, more difficult.* Use *most* to form the superlative: *most beautiful, most difficult.* Notice the use of *more* and *most* in these examples:

This book is *more difficult* than that one.
This book is the *most difficult* one I ever read.

Here is a rule of thumb to make things easier for you. To most adjectives of one or two syllables add *-er* or *-est.* Adjectives with three or more syllables take *more* or *most.*

Page 77

Adjectives and Linking Verbs

In a sentence, an adjective is often found right next to the noun or pronoun it describes (modifies). In the following sentence *heavy* modifies *schedule*:

> We have a **heavy schedule.**

However, an adjective may be separated from the word it modifies by a linking verb. For example:

> Our **schedule** is **heavy.**

The adjective is *heavy. Heavy* is separated from the noun it modifies (*schedule*) by the linking verb *is*.

> This is a **long day.**   This **day** is **long.**

The adjective in both is *long* and the word it modifies is *day*.

A. On each line of the following table one of the three adjective forms is written. Fill in the other two forms.

	Simple	*Comparative*	*Superlative*
1.	pretty		
2.		busier	
3.	familiar		
4.		hotter	
5.			saddest
6.	difficult		
7.			loveliest
8.	unusual		
9.		friendlier	
10.			most important
11.	wealthy		
12.		happier	
13.	dry		
14.		longer	
15.	powerful		
16.			easiest
17.	comparable		
18.		more fallible	
19.	weak		
20.	colorful		

Page 78   adjectives (1)

UNIT 9
adjectives (2)

Irregular Adjectives

A few adjectives form their comparatives and superlatives in an irregular manner. You are probably familiar with most of them.

A. The simple form of each irregular adjective is listed below. Using your dictionary, fill in the comparative and superlative forms. In several cases there is more than one answer.

	Simple	*Comparative*	*Superlative*
1.	bad		
2.	good		
3.	little		
4.	many or much		
5.	late		
6.	far		

Forms of Adjectives

A. In the space provided, write the proper form of the adjective in parentheses.

1. Although Mr. Smith and Mr. Jones are bright, Mr. Roberts is the (wise). _____
2. Which of this pair has the (bright) colors? _____
3. Though our Raleigh plant is large, the Durham plant is (large). _____
4. New York is the (exciting) of the two cities. _____
5. New York is the (exciting) city in the world. _____

6. She is the (tall) girl in the whole office. _____

7. The left sleeve is (long) than the right. _____

8. Of all our forty-three offices, the (large) is in Los Angeles. _____

9. Test this one, then that one, and choose the (good). _____

10. Which of the twins is the (pretty)? _____

Review

A. Some of the following sentences have errors concerning verbals. Rewrite each sentence correctly (you may have to add words). If the sentence is correct, write *C* on the line.

1. Driving down the street, the restaurant came into view.
_____

2. She wants to hastily complete the task.
_____

3. Skating gracefully, she won first place in the competition.
_____

4. He prefers to play golf and swimming on his vacation.
_____

5. Speaking softly, the audience listened to the lecturer.
_____

B. Underline the verb in each of the following sentences. If the verb is transitive, write *T* in the space provided. If the verb is intransitive, write *I*.

1. He put the mail on the desk. _____

2. The sun shines on the window. _____

3. Lay the envelope on the desk. _____

4. The secretary typed a letter to the client. _____

5. He has chosen a few samples. _____

6. She waved to her friend. _____

7. He had laid the package on the shelf. _____

8. The sign was displayed for all to see. _____

9. He rises early in the morning. _____

10. I want that piece of cake. _____

Page 80   adjectives (2)

name section date

UNIT 9
adjectives (3)

assignment

A. Underline the adjective in each of the following sentences with one line. Then underline the word each adjective modifies with two lines.

1. He picked up the heavy case.
2. She prepared a light supper.
3. The colored lights were dimmed.
4. It was a very efficient system.
5. We have complete records.
6. Our latest records show a deficit.
7. We sent an order for farm machinery.
8. He slowly walked to his first class.
9. These are first-class goods.
10. Here is our new catalogue.
11. Send me your final approval.
12. Where is my brown hat?
13. Forgive my late reply.

14. The table has a smooth finish.

15. We went horseback riding.

16. It's a very smooth-riding car.

17. This is an easy problem.

18. This problem is easy.

19. I am hungry.

20. He feels hungry.

B. In the space provided, write the proper form of the adjective in parentheses.

1. This is the (bad) snowstorm we have ever had. _____
2. He stated a (forceful) argument than she did. _____
3. The department store is (far) than the drug store. _____
4. Mrs. Jones is always the (late) person to arrive. _____
5. This movie was (good) than the one we saw last week. _____
6. The red package is (heavy) than the blue one. _____
7. She is the (happy) person in the world today. _____
8. He bought the (little) expensive car in the showroom. _____
9. She is the (graceful) dancer in the ballet class. _____
10. This speaker is (interesting) than the preceding one. _____
11. That is the (good) restaurant in town. _____
12. My friend is the (young) of his three brothers. _____
13. The pink dress is (attractive) than the green one. _____
14. This is the (sad) story I have read. _____
15. Susan is (lazy) than her brother. _____

If a word will take the ending *-er* or *-est* or if it will fit into either blank in the sentence *The ___ house is very ___*, the word is an adjective.

UNIT 10
using adjectives (1)

Introduction

To use any adjective correctly you will have to pay careful attention to the sentence in which it is placed. It is important to be able to identify the noun or pronoun which is modified. In a comparison, it is important to know what is being compared. In this unit we will discuss specific adjectives which can be troublesome and we will help you to learn their correct usage.

In your work, you will need to know when to capitalize adjectives. If an adjective is derived from a proper noun it should be capitalized. We call this type of adjective a *proper adjective*. Words like *American, Asiatic,* and *Victorian* are examples.

Some proper adjectives are no longer thought of in connection with the original noun and therefore are not capitalized. Such adjectives include *morocco binding, oriental rug,* and *jersey wool.*

When an adjective is composed of two or more words it is called a *compound adjective*. Examples include *well bred, first class,* and *up to date.* Compound adjectives are generally hyphenated when they immediately precede the noun they describe; they are generally not hyphenated when they come after the noun.

> We sell **first-class** products.
> The products we sell are **first class.**

Compound adjectives are often formed by joining a numeral with words of measure like *inch, foot, mile, pound, month,* and *quart.* The basic rule for hyphenating compound adjectives still holds true:

> a **three-foot** ruler   a ruler **three feet** long

Note that in the hyphenated adjectives that precede the noun the unit of measure is always singular:

> a five-**pound** cake *but* a cake of five **pounds**

Page 83

There are a few compound adjectives that are always hyphenated regardless of their position in a sentence. Included are all compound adjectives formed with *self:*

> He is a **self-made** man.
> The truth is **self-evident.**

Also included in this group are numerical adjectives from twenty-one through ninety-nine:

> We celebrated our **twenty-fifth** anniversary.

Sometimes an entire phrase will be used to modify a noun. This phrase is called an *adjective phrase*. Here is a sentence with an adjective phrase:

> The desk **with the steel legs** is sturdy.

The phrase *with the steel legs* modifies *desk*.

You should always place an adjective phrase as close as possible to the word it modifies. Failure to do so can result in strange sentences like this one:

> They delivered the piano to the **woman with mahogany legs.**

The phrase *with mahogany legs* should follow the noun *piano*.

When in doubt about hyphenating or spelling, use your dictionary.

Other and **else:** When a member of a group is compared with the rest of the group it is necessary to exclude that member by the use of the word *other* or the word *else* as follows:

> I am smarter than any **other** person in my class.
> I am smarter than anyone **else** in my class.

A. Rewrite these sentences in the space provided, using the words *else* or *other*.

EXAMPLE: She is more creative than any person in the art class.
She is more creative than any other person in the art class.

1. My son is smaller than any boy in his class.

2. Mr. Smith is shrewder than anyone in his department.

3. Mr. Jones is more popular than anyone.

4. This is the best and most efficient of any system used today.

5. More level-headed than any man in his company, John was promoted.

UNIT 10
using adjectives (2)

Less and **fewer:** *Less* should be used to refer to items measured in bulk. *Fewer* should be used to refer to items counted separately.

> **Less** coal was mined this year.
> **Fewer** men applied for the job than we anticipated.

A. For each sentence below, underline the correct word in parentheses.

1. They delivered (less, fewer) coal than we had ordered.
2. They delivered (less, fewer) tons of coal than we had ordered.
3. There were (less, fewer) than ten customers today.
4. We can do the same amount of work with (less, fewer) secretaries.
5. Your firm has sent (less, fewer) orders than anticipated.
6. There is (less, fewer) unemployment than anticipated.
7. This air conditioner uses (less, fewer) electricity than any other model.
8. This air conditioner uses (less, fewer) kilowatts of electricity than any other model.
9. This typewriter weighs (less, fewer) than twenty pounds.
10. (Less, Fewer) than ten people showed up.

One another and **each other:** *One another* refers to three or more persons or things. *Each other* refers to only two persons or things.

> The three men know **one another.**
> The two men knew **each other.**

A. For each sentence below, underline the correct word in parentheses.

1. The two men spoke to (each other, one another).
2. The committee members spoke to (each other, one another) until it was time to convene.
3. We are acquainted with (each other, one another), he and I.
4. The men in the mob prodded (each other, one another) to greater violence.
5. The two airmen helped (each other, one another) survive in the jungle.

Only: Always place the word *only* as close as possible to the word it modifies so that its meaning is absolutely clear.

> I paid **only** eight dollars.

Page 85

A. Indicate the proper placement of the word *only* for each of the following sentences. Cross out the word *only* if it is incorrectly placed. Use a caret and write *only* in the proper place.

1. The President only signed the first bill.

2. He only saw three familiar faces.

3. I only met him twice.

4. We only filed our applications one day late.

5. This hat only cost three dollars.

First and **last:** When using the word *first* or the word *last* to modify a number, always place it directly before that number.

>The **first eight** pages have been typed.
>The **last six** people arrived late.

A. Indicate the proper placement of *first* or *last* for each of the following sentences.

1. We enjoyed the two last weeks.
2. I don't understand the eight first pages.
3. We haven't heard from him for the three last days.
4. We have read all but the eight last pages.
5. Only the six first people were admitted.

Farther, further, farthest, and **furthest:** Sometimes these forms of the simple adjective *far* are confusing. The words *farther* and *farthest* should be used when an actual physical distance is thought of.

>Our car will travel **farther** on less gas.

Use *further* and *furthest* in all other situations.

>Study this chapter **further.**

A. For each sentence, underline the correct word in parentheses.

1. He threw the ball (farther, further) than I.
2. He sat in the chair (farthest, furthest) from the chairman.
3. I will go to the (farthest, furthest) place in the world for you.
4. (Further, farther) than that, I cannot go in compromising with you.
5. If we delve (farther, further), we will find the solution.

UNIT 10

using adjectives (3)

Articles

There are three adjectives which have the special name *articles*. The articles are *a*, *an*, and *the*. Whether to use *a* or *an* depends on the sound of the next word in the sentence. When the next word begins with a *consonant sound*, you use *a*. A consonant sound is the sound of any letter in the alphabet except the vowel sounds *a, e, i, o,* and *u*. You use *an* wherever a word begins with a *vowel sound.*

a boy **an** apple
a man **an** orange

When selecting *a* or *an* to precede a noun, carefully check the sound of that noun. Note that you say: *a happy boy,* but *an honest man.* Although *h* is a consonant, it is silent in the word *honest.* While you say *an umbrella,* you say *a university* because the *u* in *university* begins with a *y* sound like the *y* in *you.*

A. In the spaces provided write either *a* or *an*, whichever is correct.

1. _____ man wearing _____ unusual jacket left _____ package.
2. _____ humorist is _____ human being with _____ peculiar sense of humor.
3. _____ understanding of all operations in our plant is _____ necessity for _____ foreman.
4. _____ hour before dawn is _____ inhuman hour for _____ human being to be awakened.
5. _____ union leader should be _____ honest man, for to lead _____ union is _____ undertaking of great responsibility.

Occasionally you will be faced with a problem of whether to repeat the article when you are listing a series of things. For example:

The red and (the) white coats are on sale.

Should you use the extra *the*? This depends upon what you mean. If each coat is part red and part white then omit the extra *the*. For the sake of clarity, you could use hyphens here to express your meaning:

The **red-and-white** coats are on sale.

If there are two types of coats—one all red and the other all white—then add the extra *the:*

>**The** red and **the** white coats are on sale.

Study these sentences and explanations:

>The President and the Chairman arrived. (*Two* men.)
>The President and Chairman arrived. (*One* man holding both positions.)
>The steel and the plastic cabinets are in place. (Some cabinets are all steel and some, all plastic.)
>The steel and plastic cabinets are in place. (Cabinets of part steel and part plastic.)

B. Indicate the necessary changes to make the sentences correct. Use a caret and add *the* or cross out *the* where it is incorrect.

1. The secretary and vice-president met at noon.

2. He was elected to be both the vice-president and the secretary.

3. The car has a blue and a white finish.

4. We have in stock two cabinets, a chromium and aluminum one.

5. She wore a red and a green sweater.

Later and **latter:** *Later* is the comparative form of the adjective *late* and refers to time.

>I shall be there **later.**

Latter means the second of two; it is usually used as the opposite of *former,* which means the first of two.

>Jones and Smith were both successful—the former through luck; the **latter** through hard work.

A. For each sentence below, underline the correct word in parentheses.

1. The (later, latter) we meet tonight, the less time we will have.
2. The (later, latter) part of the sermon contained some powerful points.
3. The former speaker introduced the guest; the (later, latter) spoke at length.
4. The two men spoke. The former said: "It is (later, latter) than you think."
5. The speech was given (later, latter) than I had expected.

UNIT 10
using adjectives (4)

assignment

A. The following sentences concern capitalizing and hyphenating adjectives. For each sentence, underline the correct word in parentheses.

1. The (American, american) Indian created (well-made, well made) tools.
2. The (Victorian, victorian) age occurred in the '80's.
3. A (Persian, persian) rug may be very valuable.
4. He heard (Martial, martial) music on the radio.
5. He was a (well-intentioned, well intentioned) worker who made mistakes.
6. The fact that he cannot perform the work is (self-evident, self evident).
7. A (first-rate, first rate) mechanic is difficult to get.
8. The battalion put up a (last-ditch, last ditch) effort.
9. This pie is obviously (home made, home-made).
10. In this office we need workers who are (well-disciplined, well disciplined).

B. Each of the sentences below is incorrect because of a misplaced modifier. Rewrite these sentences.

1. People cannot fail to notice vast changes in business methods who are in touch with business offices.

2. We saw the new building walking down East Shore Drive.

Page 89

3. The soldier saddled his horse who was wearing a new uniform.

4. Take the book to the man with the beautiful leather binding.

5. The dog ran toward his master wagging his tail.

C. This letter contains many errors in the use of adjectives. Cross out each error and write the correction above it.

Dear Mr. White:

Have you heard about our sale on phonograph records? This sale is excitinger and spectacularer than any sale in this city's history.

Only during the two first weeks we have sold no less than 10,000 records in each of our two stores. You might be interested to know that the South Street store has sold the greatest number of records even though the store is furthest from the heart of town. This is a extremely unusual development.

We would be very grateful if you would visit our store. You can't miss it, walking down Sixth Avenue toward Elm. Mr. Johnson, our manager, and his assistant, Mr. Roberts, are very anxious to see you. I'm sure you three will enjoy chatting with each other.

Perhaps you will explain to these men why they have least sales than the South Street store. We want you to give them a honest opinion. See if you can help them catch up and surpass the South Street store during the three last weeks of the sale.

Sincerely,

UNIT 11
adverbs (1)

Introduction

An *adverb* is a word that describes or modifies a verb. An adverb also can modify an adjective or another adverb. Here are three sentences using adverbs:

The ship sailed **swiftly.**

The adverb *swiftly* modifies the verb *sailed.*

Broadway is an **extremely** wide street.

The adverb *extremely* modifies the adjective *wide.*

The old man walked **very** slowly.

The adverb *very* modifies the adverb *slowly.*

An adverb is a word that tells you *how, when, where,* or *how much.*

The book was printed **carefully.**

The adverb *carefully* describes *how* the book was printed.

The order was shipped **promptly.**

The adverb *promptly* describes *when* the order was shipped.

The officials came **here.**

The adverb *here* tells *where* the officials came.

They were **very** pleased.

The adverb *very* tells *how much* they were pleased.

You form most adverbs from adjectives by adding *-ly:*

Adjective	*Adverb*
swift	swiftly
careful	carefully
familiar	familiarly
sole	solely

On the job you will have to choose between using an adjective or an adverb in many sentences. Here is a simple rule to follow: Use an adverb to modify an action verb. Use an adjective after a linking verb.
Look at this sentence:

The fire burned **fiercely.**

Page 91

Burned is an action verb; therefore, we use the adverb *fiercely*.

>The tiger is **fierce.**

In the lesson on adjectives you learned that an adjective can be separated from the word it modifies by a linking verb. *Fierce* modifies *tiger* in the above sentence.

>The tiger looks **fierce.**

Looks as used in this sentence is a linking verb. *Looks* could be replaced by *is*. So again we use the adjective *fierce* because it follows a linking verb and really describes the subject-noun *tiger* and not the verb *looks*.

>He looked (*fierce, fiercely*) for the missing wallet.

Is *looked,* as used here, an action or a linking verb? Could it be replaced by *was?* No. Therefore *looked* requires the adverb *fiercely*.

Adverbs may be compared just as adjectives may be. To one- or two-syllable words add *-er* and *-est: soon, sooner, soonest.* Adverbs that are longer are usually formed by using the words *more* and *most: happily, more happily, most happily.*

Remember to use the comparative form when comparing two, and the superlative form when comparing three or more.

>I will arrive *earlier* than he.
>I arrived *earlier* than any of them.
>Of them all, I arrived *earliest.*

A. Underline the adverb in each of the following sentences with one line. Then underline the word it modifies with two lines.

1. The plane traveled swiftly.
2. We are very much pleased to hear from you.
3. We walked quietly to the side.
4. Quickly he leaped into his car.
5. The matter is entirely finished.
6. No two men are completely alike.
7. This occurrence is most unfortunate.
8. We strongly urge you to accept this offer.
9. Recheck thoroughly all outgoing mail.
10. They came here much later than expected.
11. He was essentially interested in securing a patent.
12. We were unusually surprised by his work.
13. All our customers are comfortably dressed when they leave us.
14. Watch this maneuver intently.
15. Mr. Jones arrived at the meeting exactly at the appointed hour.
16. The boy went in the pool cautiously.
17. The grass grows quickly in this weather.
18. This project was finished carelessly.
19. She will happily complete the work.
20. The traveler stood wearily by the bus stop.

UNIT 11
adverbs (2)

Forming Adverbs

In spelling adverbs, add *-ly* to the adjective. This applies to words ending in *-al* and *-e* as well as other adjectives (*lovely, initially*).

Exceptions to the rule about retaining the *-e* when adding *-ly* are *truly, duly,* and *wholly.*

A. In the space next to each adjective below, write the equivalent adverb.

1. separate _____
2. authoritative _____
3. official _____
4. real _____
5. extreme _____
6. principal _____
7. helpful _____
8. whole _____
9. cordial _____
10. sole _____
11. substantial _____
12. scarce _____

When the adjective ends in *y,* to form the adverb change the *y* to *i* and add *ly.*

B. Write the equivalent adverb for each adjective below.

1. busy _____
2. happy _____
3. satisfactory _____
4. temporary _____
5. primary _____
6. extraordinary _____
7. ready _____
8. lazy _____
9. hungry _____
10. angry _____
11. steady _____
12. sleepy _____

When the adjective ends in *-able* or *-ible,* to form the adverb drop the final *-e* and add *-y.*

C. Write the equivalent adverb for each adjective below.

1. noticeable _____
2. considerable _____
3. forcible _____
4. horrible _____
5. considerable _____
6. peaceable _____
7. changeable _____
8. sensible _____
9. comfortable _____
10. legible _____
11. miserable _____
12. profitable _____

Review

A. Each classified advertisement below contains several adjectives. Underline each adjective with one line. Then underline the word each adjective modifies with two lines.

1. SECRETARY—Enthusiastic woman with secretarial training and experience is sought for challenging position as secretary to over-burdened executive in theatrical field.
2. RECEPTIONIST-STENO—We have an excellent position available in our Sales Department. Your competent skills and pleasant personality will make this an interesting opportunity. Attractive surroundings with good salary and outstanding benefits.
3. SALES MANAGER—Need bright individual to manage sales operation in small store with fine reputation in suburban community.
4. REAL ESTATE SALESMAN NEEDED—New office looking for aggressive person with professional attitude and knowledge of real estate business. Generous commissions; sensible schedule.

B. In the space provided, write the proper form of the adjective in parentheses.

1. The weather is (warm) here than it is in New York. _____
2. Do you see the (bright) star in the sky? _____
3. Charles is the (intelligent) student in the class. _____
4. Susan is (energetic) than her sister. _____
5. Which city is (far), Dallas or Houston? _____
6. We would like to see the (late) model in stock. _____
7. Sam is the (fast) runner on the team. _____
8. The factory is (busy) than it has been in years. _____
9. This is the (difficult) decision he has had to make. _____
10. John is (short) than Jim. _____

Unique means the only one of its kind and therefore has no comparative or superlative form—nothing can be more unique or most unique. The same is true of *perfect;* nothing can be more or most perfect.

UNIT 11

adverbs (3)

assignment

A. For each sentence below decide whether to use an adjective or an adverb. Write the proper form of the word in parentheses in the space provided.

1. Candy tastes (sweet). _____
2. He tasted the mixture (careful). _____
3. Return the merchandise as (quick) as possible. _____
4. He is very (content). _____
5. The situation seems (bad). _____
6. I am (extreme) tired from my long journey. _____
7. The plant grew more and more (quick). _____
8. The whole garden smells (sweet). _____
9. We (certain) hope you are comfortable. _____
10. We feel he has been (extraordinary) competent at his task. _____
11. Ordinarily the bell tolls (soft), but today it sounds (loud). _____
12. Our situation has grown (bad). _____
13. She looks (beautiful). _____
14. We can accomplish our goals (easy). _____
15. He has done (good, well) in his new post. _____
16. He will arrive more (quick) if he takes the plane. _____

17. The food was (plentiful). _____
18. He drank (deep) of the wine. _____
19. He has done (easy) twice as much work as Smith. _____
20. You (sure) must be proud of what you have accomplished. _____

B. For each sentence below decide whether to use an adjective or an adverb. Write the proper form of the word in parentheses in the space provided.

1. Our product is becoming more and more (desirable) in its line. _____
2. Mr. Jones became (angry) and threatened his employee (loud). _____
3. He feels (indignant) because he cannot attend. _____
4. The whole story sounds (strange). _____
5. You are paying an (extreme) large amount. _____
6. We will (glad) repay your losses. _____
7. This is a very (poor) constructed problem. _____
8. The river flowed (rapid). _____
9. Do business conditions look (bad) to you? _____
10. Rewrite the entire page (correct). _____
11. Please have a clerk file these papers (quick). _____
12. Mr. Roberts certainly is a (quick) thinker. _____
13. When faced with an emergency, Mr. Roberts thought (quick). _____
14. There is no doubt about Mr. Roberts' being (quick). _____
15. Mr. Smith tasted his soup (hungry). _____

Remember the exception to the *i* before *e* rule: when these two letters stand for the sound "ay," as in *weigh, deign,* and *sleigh,* the *e* comes first.

UNIT 12
using adverbs (1)

Introduction

To use adverbs correctly you need a knowledge of the relationship between adjectives and adverbs. You also need to know the distinction between action and linking verbs.

Whether you use an adverb or an adjective in a specific sentence is determined by the job that word has to do. In this unit you will learn about specific adverbs which are often confused with similar adjectives. Sometimes these words are confused because they sound nearly the same, such as the adverb *surely* and the adjective *sure*. Sometimes they are confused because of similar meanings, such as *well* and *good*.

Words expressing the idea of *no*, such as *not*, are called *negatives*. In using English correctly, it is important that you avoid using two negatives in a sentence. Here is an example of this erroneous use of negatives which we call the *double negative*:

> They **don't** know **nothing.**

This sentence contains two negatives, *don't* and *nothing*. Each of these negatives destroys the other. By eliminating either of them we get a correct sentence:

> They know **nothing.**
> They **don't** know anything.

Good and **well:** *Good* is an adjective. *Well* is usually an adverb.

> Dinner tasted **good.**

Since *tasted* is a linking verb, we use the adjective *good*. *Tasted* really means *was*.

Here is another sentence:

> He performed **well.**

Since *performed* is an action verb, we use the adverb *well*.

Page 97

The only time that *well* is used as an adjective is when it means *healthy*. In this case, *well* can be used after a linking verb.

He is **well.**   He feels **well.**   He looks **well.**

The comparative and superlative forms of both *good* and *well* are *better* and *best*.

A. In the space provided, write the correct word.

1. You did the job very (good, well). _____
2. You did a very (good, well) job. _____
3. It sounds (good, well) to me. _____
4. You look (good, well) in your new suit. _____
5. He performs (good, well) on the piano. _____
6. The job was done quite (good, well). _____
7. The proposition sounds (good, well). _____
8. We feel confident you shall do (good, well) in your new position. _____
9. Though he was sick, he is now completely (good, well). _____
10. He was extremely (good, well) in the part of Hamlet. _____
11. The flower smells (good, well). _____
12. He works (good, well). _____
13. She wrote the report (good, well). _____
14. He gave a (good, well) speech. _____
15. The hospital reports that he is doing (good, well). _____

UNIT 12

using adverbs (2)

Most and **almost:** A test to determine whether to use *most* or *almost* is to try to substitute the word *nearly*. If *nearly* fits, then *almost* would be proper also. If *nearly* does not fit, *most* should be used.

    Almost all the orders were sent.

The word *nearly* will make sense in the sentence above. Therefore, use *almost* rather than *most*.

    Who had the **most** errors?

The word *nearly* will not make sense here. Therefore, use *most*.

A. In the space provided, write the correct word.

1. These are (most, almost) all of the supplies that are left. _____
2. We found that (most, almost) people did not answer. _____
3. He is (most, almost) as good as his competitor. _____
4. (Most, Almost) everything was finished by noon. _____
5. (Most, Almost) of the time we work quite hard. _____
6. It was (most, almost) too good to be true. _____
7. We feel that (most, almost) of our staff is doing a top-notch job. _____
8. It seems that (most, almost) all of the men answered our plea. _____
9. He can sell (most, almost) as well as any of our other salesmen. _____
10. (Most, Almost) anyone who dresses well can look attractive. _____
11. It was (most, almost) too late to catch the train. _____
12. (Most, Almost) everyone was present. _____
13. (Most, Almost) all of the merchandise was returned. _____

Page 99

14. It was evident that (most, almost) half the group would veto the measure.

15. She indicated that it was (most, almost) time to leave.

Double Negatives

These words are negative in themselves and should never be used with the word *not: scarcely, hardly, never, neither,* and *but.*

> We can **scarcely** see you in the fog.
> We could **hardly** have decided otherwise.
> It could **never** happen here.
> It was **neither** of them.
> I understand all **but** one of them.

A. Rewrite the following letter, correcting all double-negative expressions.

Dear Mr. Bronson:

Mr. Marshall from your office hasn't scarcely visited us more than a few times in the past few months. We certainly hope that we haven't done nothing to offend him. After all, we haven't hardly started in our association with your firm, and we certainly wouldn't want to do nothing that would jeopardize our fine relationship.

Sincerely,

UNIT 12

using adverbs (3)

Real and **very:** *Real* is an adjective meaning *genuine*. *Very* is an adverb meaning *extremely*. When faced with a choice of using *real* or *very*, substitute *genuine* or *extremely*. If *genuine* fits, *real* is correct. If *extremely* fits, *very* is correct.

    I am **very** (extremely) pleased.
    It gives me **real** (genuine) pleasure to introduce the next speaker.

A. In the space provided, write the correct word.

1. These diamonds are (real, very). _____
2. He was (real, very) pleased to meet them. _____
3. It gives us (real, very) satisfaction. _____
4. We are (real, very) sorry we cannot comply. _____
5. After a day's work he was (real, very) tired. _____
6. Were the (real, very) situation known, there might be a scandal. _____
7. The teachers were (real, very) concerned about her grades. _____
8. This matter is (real, very) important. _____
9. We have (real, very) valid reasons for our stand. _____
10. Are you (real, very) well sure of your facts? _____
11. I am (real, very) interested in these plans. _____
12. I am (real, very) happy to work here. _____
13. We are (real, very) pleased with the outcome. _____
14. It was a (real, very) antique. _____
15. It was a (real, very) wonderful movie. _____

Page 101

Unnecessary Adverbs

Sometimes the adverbial meaning of *how, when, where,* or *how much* is expressed in other words in the sentence.

Recopy this page **over.**

In this sentence the word *over* is unnecessary as *recopy* means *to copy (over) again.*

They must cooperate **together.**

Since *cooperate* means *to act or work together,* the use of *together* is unnecessary.

A. If the adverb is used unnecessarily, write it in the space provided. If there is no unnecessary adverb, write *C* for correct.

1. Please repaint this wall again. _____
2. Exit out this way. _____
3. Return those papers back to me. _____
4. Cooperate together with your associates. _____
5. Please repeat the letter again. _____
6. Let us reconvene again on Monday morning. _____
7. In re-examining the ledger, they discovered the error. _____
8. We want nations to coexist together in harmony. _____
9. The new fan has conquered over all competition. _____
10. Try to cooperate as fully as you can. _____
11. I shall repeat the question again. _____
12. He has returned back from Europe. _____
13. Erase this out. _____
14. He returned the bills to me. _____
15. She reviewed the directions again. _____

using adverbs (4)

UNIT 12

Compound Words Confused with Adverbs

Sometimes compound expressions beginning with *all* are confused with adverbs beginning with *al*. If you examine these compound expressions you will see that their meanings are quite different from the adverbs they resemble.

All together means *many combined;* *altogether* means *completely.*

> They worked **all together** until they were **altogether** satisfied.

All ways means *every manner;* *always* means *forever.*

> **Always** remember that there are **all ways** of reaching happiness.

All ready means *completely prepared;* *already* means *previously.*

> The employees were **all ready** at five o'clock, though some had **already** punched out.

Most authorities consider that *alright* is poor usage, so use *all right* instead.

A. In the space provided, write the correct word or words.

1. He is (all together, altogether) wrong in his approach. _____
2. In (all ways, always) this edition seems superior. _____
3. Many students have (all ready, already) taken some college courses. _____
4. (All together, Altogether) I counted thirty-three people. _____
5. It's (all right, alright) to leave before the bell. _____
6. The new firm failed (all together, altogether). _____
7. He is in (all ways, always) a model employee. _____
8. I think the bank tellers are (all ready, already) to end their day's work. _____
9. Conditions are neither (all right, alright) nor (all wrong, alwrong.) _____
10. (All right, Alright), you may go when you are (all ready, already.) _____

Page 103

Sure and **surely:** The adjective *sure* means *confident* or *certain;* the adverb *surely* means *certainly* or *undoubtedly.*

      He is quite **sure** of himself.
      He **surely** did an effective job.

A. In the space provided, write the correct word.

1. (Sure, Surely) I'll go with you. _____
2. I am (sure, surely) happy that prices have leveled off. _____
3. She (sure, surely) is the best swimmer on the team. _____
4. Mr. Johnson is (sure, surely) the man for the job. _____
5. Mrs. Smith is (sure, surely) her friend will arrive soon. _____

Review

A. On each line of the following table is written one of the three adverbial forms. Fill in the other two forms. Use your dictionary to help you with the spelling.

	Simple	*Comparative*	*Superlative*
1.	powerfully		
2.		more sadly	
3.	swiftly		
4.			earliest
5.		more sincerely	
6.	soon		
7.			best
8.	promptly		
9.		more carefully	
10.			latest

B. In the space provided, write the proper form of the adverb in parentheses.

EXAMPLE: She completed her tasks (easily) than her sister.   more easily

1. The boy worked (carefully) than his friend. _____
2. The couple will arrive (early) than you expect. _____
3. He runs (quickly) of all his teammates. _____
4. She responded (soon) than any of them. _____
5. He spoke (sharply) to his neighbor. _____

name　　　　　　　　　　　　　section　　　　　　　　　　　　　date

UNIT 12

using adverbs (5)

assignment

A. The first half of a letter appears on this page, and the concluding half on page 106. The letter contains many errors in the use of adverbs. Cross out each error and write the correction above it.

Dear Mr. Spears:

　　It was a genuine pleasure to see you at the Acme Convention in Pittsburgh. I thought you looked real good, considering the seriousness of your recent illness. We sure hope you enjoyed your visit to Pittsburgh and that everything was alright there.

　　The Acme Company is growing very quick. Last year's sales are a tiny fraction of our anticipated sales this year. Our situation is growing more better every day. I am certain that we can easily accomplish the goals we set for ourselves in Pittsburgh.

The following is the continuation of the letter begun on page 105. Cross out each error and write the correction above it.

One situation I feel badly about is the growth of competition in the South. If one looks close at sales figures in the South, he will see that the rate of increase does not look as well as we had first thought. I am real concerned with this problem.

On the other hand, our Western office has done extremely good. They are real quick rising to Number One position in the nation. I wish that our other offices followed our advice as complete and thoroughly as they do.

By the way, John Raymond feels indignantly because he was not chosen as a speaker in Pittsburgh. Even though his speaking is real poorly, he is an important person. While I am not positive that there will be time for him at the next convention, I am most surely that we can squeeze him in.

Please write and let us know if you are feeling weller.

Sincerely,

UNIT 13

prepositions (1)

Introduction

A *preposition* is a word that connects a noun or pronoun with the body of the sentence. The noun or pronoun that the preposition connects to the body of the sentence is called the *object* of that preposition. Words such as *of, at, in, on,* and *between* are prepositions.

> **of John**—*John* is the object of the preposition *of*
> **at the time**—*time* is the object of the preposition *at*
> **in the room**—*room* is the object of the preposition *in*
> **on the way**—*way* is the object of the preposition *on*
> **between you and me**—*you* and *me* are the objects of the preposition *between*

A phrase that is introduced by a preposition is called a *prepositional phrase*.

> I arrived **on time.**

In this sentence *on time* is a prepositional phrase. *On* is the preposition; *time* is the object of the preposition.

Here is a list of the most common prepositions:

about	before	down	on	toward
above	behind	during	over	under
across	below	except	regarding	underneath
after	beneath	for	respecting	until
against	between	from	since	up
along	beyond	in	through	upon
among	but	into	throughout	with
around	by	of	till	within
at	concerning	off	to	without

In addition, there are a number of familiar word groups that are used as though the whole group were a preposition:

as to	by way of	from beyond	in reference to
as for	contrary to	instead of	on account of
as regards	devoid of	in place of	to the extent of
apart from	from out	in regard to	with respect to

In this unit you will be working with many of these prepositions and learning to use them correctly.

Some prepositions are used unnecessarily. You should learn to recognize these prepositions so that your sentences are clear and uncluttered. Following are sentences which illustrate this point. The unnecessary prepositions are in boldface.

> Where are you going **to?**
> Where is your home **at?**
> I cannot help **from** expressing my gratitude.
> I want **for** you to see this.
> **Up** until yesterday, I would have agreed.
> In two weeks, it will be over **with.**

On the other hand, in writing and speaking it is easy to omit prepositions that are necessary. The following sentences are correct; the prepositions indicated are often omitted in error.

> What type **of** work do you do?
> Tell him what style **of** cabinet we want.
> I was graduated **from** high school two years ago.

Recognizing Prepositions

A. In each sentence below underline all prepositions with one line. Then underline the objects of those prepositions with two lines.

1. Did you hear of the trouble at the office?
2. Mr. Atwood was in his office when you called.
3. The reputation of Empire Fans has been built on high standards and fair dealings at all times.
4. Between you and me, I feel certain that one of the representatives will call at your office within a week.
5. In regard to any orders from your firm, we feel sure of our ability to fill them in time for your fall shipment.
6. With respect to your claim for damages, we are certain of a recovery to the extent of $3,000.
7. Contrary to our expectations, you will be refused a passport for the duration of the present emergency.
8. They have agreed among themselves to honor, without any question, all of the demands made by our client.
9. Against all odds, we have succeeded beyond expectation in our endeavor to enlist support for our cause.
10. Instead of being discouraged by his failure, he seemed to gain the strength of a lion in all his subsequent attempts.
11. Walking into the hall, the President of the United States and the members of his cabinet were greeted by the complete silence of the assembled guests.
12. In spite of his aversion to the tactics of high-pressure salesmen, Mr. Jones was so impressed by this young man that he agreed to buy his full line of goods.
13. In regard to the order, the duplicate was used in place of the original.
14. He walked into the room and sat down.
15. He got out of his car and went into the office.

UNIT 13

prepositions (2)

From, than, and **with:** Always use the word *from* after the word *different* when you mean that something is *different from* something else. A thing is never *different than* something else.

My theory is **different from** the one held by my boss.

Use *from* after the word *differ,* unless differ is used as a verb meaning *disagree.* In that case use the preposition *with*.

This may **differ from** what you had thought.
We **differ with** your conclusion.

A. In the space provided, write the correct preposition, either *from* or *with*.

1. My idea is different _____ yours.
2. Our course may differ _____ what you had expected.
3. Approach the topic differently _____ the way you did last time.
4. The Board differed _____ the advice of the Director.
5. His designs are no different _____ the designs he showed last time.
6. What we differ _____ is your desire for haste.
7. The course they chose was different _____ that outlined in the manual.
8. Our attorneys differ _____ this report's interpretation of the facts.
9. Have you nothing different _____ what you showed me last week?
10. The new car models are very different _____ the old ones.
11. This year's fashions differ greatly _____ last year's.
12. I told him that I begged to differ _____ him.
13. Our product is not only different _____ our competitor's, it is superior.
14. The members of the committee differed _____ each other.
15. How is a lion different _____ a tiger?

Page 109

In and **into:** *In* means *within*. *Into* means *from the outside to within*. *Into* expresses an action of moving from one place (outside) to another place (inside). *In* expresses no action.

>The director is **in** the room.
>The director went **into** the room.

The words *in* or *into* in the same sentence may change the meaning completely.

>He ran **in** the ring.
>He ran **into** the ring.

A. In the space provided, write the correct preposition, either *in* or *into*.

1. He walked _____ the room from the hall.
2. Behind a closed door, he paced back and forth _____ his office all day.
3. There are some fascinating articles _____ today's newspaper.
4. It doesn't take much to get _____ a fight with him.
5. What sort of work would you like to get _____?
6. Promotion is rapid, once you have established a name _____ this field.
7. He opened the door and rushed _____ his office.
8. I would tear this contract _____ a thousand little pieces if I could.
9. Do you think you can get _____ the public relations field?
10. You can work your way _____ the confidence of your superior only by intense effort.

Off and **of:** There are two simple rules to remember about using *off* and *of*. First, do not use the word *of* after the word *off*.

>The radio fell **off** the table.

Second, do not use *of* when you mean *have*. *Of* often is incorrectly used in place of *have* after *might, must, could, should,* or *would*.

>I might **have** gone.

A. In the space provided, write the correct word or words.

1. Money was stolen (off of, from) the safe. _____
2. The child fell (off of, off) the chair. _____
3. I could (have, of) completed the job by noon. _____
4. They took the receipts (off of, from) me. _____
5. With luck he might (have, of) pulled through. _____

UNIT 13

prepositions (3)

Prepositions Requiring Special Attention

There are several prepositions which are particularly troublesome. They are *over, to, during, for, at, around, about, beside,* and *besides.* In order to help you learn when to use these prepositions correctly we present the following helpful hints.

Over means *on top of* or *in excess of.* Do not use *over* for *to, at, during,* or *for.* These sentences are correct:

> Come **to** my house tonight.
> Let's have the meeting **at** my home.
> We held the meeting **during** the weekend.

At indicates location. *To* indicates motion.

> I was **at** a meeting last night.
> I went **to** her graduation.

Do not confuse the adverb *too* (meaning *also* or *excessively*) or the numeral *two* (2) with the preposition *to*.

> There are **too** many people to give out only **two** prizes.

Around means *circular. About* means *approximately.*

> He just walked **around** the block.
> I'll be at the bank **about** an hour from now.

Beside means *by the side of. Besides* means *in addition to.*

> He sat down **beside** her.
> The office will send a supervisor **besides** the typist and me.

A. In the space provided, write the correct word.

1. I was (at, to) her graduation. _____

2. Too much has been said (to, too) the public about the two world powers. _____

3. Will they come (over, to) the school for the dance? _____

Page 111

4. He went (at, to) the anniversary party. _____

5. Mrs. Jones will arrive (around, about) two o'clock. _____

6. He ran (around, about) the track. _____

7. Will you sit (beside, besides) me at dinner? _____

8. No one will be there (beside, besides) us two. _____

9. He worked on the accounts (over, during) the weekend. _____

10. (Beside, Besides) all other considerations, the Treasurer should be present.

Review

A. In the space provided, write the correct adverb.

1. He was extremely (good, well) in school today. _____
2. The research report sounds (good, well). _____
3. It appears that (almost, most) all the members are present. _____
4. (Most, Almost) of the people enjoyed the play. _____
5. She looked (real, very) attractive in the green dress. _____
6. The painting is (real, very) pretty. _____
7. It gives us (real, very) pleasure to present our speaker. _____
8. The method seems (altogether, all together) wrong. _____
9. (All together, Altogether) we have nine chairs. _____
10. Are you (already, all ready) to serve dinner? _____
11. We have (already, all ready) given her the gift. _____
12. She is (always, all ways) on time. _____
13. In (always, all ways) she does her work well. _____
14. She (sure, surely) is a model patient. _____
15. I am (sure, surely) the car has been repaired. _____
16. Is he here (all ready, already)? _____
17. Is it (all right, alright) to write it as two words? _____
18. Did they come singly or were they (altogether, all together)? _____
19. Typing this letter is (real, very) difficult. _____
20. I hope you come back (real, very) soon. _____

name   section   date

UNIT 13

prepositions (4)

assignment

A. Underline each unnecessary preposition and list it in the space provided. If the sentence is correct, write *C* on the line.

EXAMPLE: Get the books off of the desk.   of

1. This is the place where I am going.   _____
2. Do you know where Mr. Smith is at?   _____
3. Did the packages fall off of the shelves?   _____
4. Here is a copy of the plans you ordered.   _____
5. We wanted for him to receive the prize.   _____
6. Up until last week we had not received any report.   _____
7. Together we can seek out a solution.   _____
8. It's a relief that summer is over with.   _____
9. By the end of the summer your shipment will be ready.   _____
10. Open up all the windows.   _____
11. I didn't remember of having received the bill.   _____
12. If I'd of known the answer, I could have won the contest.   _____
13. In another few minutes it will be done with.   _____
14. Of our many customers, you have been one of our most pleasant.   _____
15. Where are you going to?   _____

Page 113

To make looking up unfamiliar words in the dictionary easier, become familiar with the letters that sometimes stand for various consonant sounds: *ph* may stand for the sound /f/ (*phonograph*) at the beginning of a word; *gh* stands for the sound /f/ only in the middle or at the end of a word. *Ps* may stand for the sound /s/ (*psychiatry*), as may *sc* (*sciatica*). *Pn* may stand for the sound /n/ (*pneumatic*).

B. In the space provided, write the correct word or words.

1. I had a fine time (over, at) my friend's house. _____
2. Frank sat down (beside, besides) his friend. _____
3. What (type, type of) suit are you going to buy? _____
4. I'll be there (during, over) the holidays. _____
5. (Beside, Besides) my employer and me, who else is invited? _____
6. He ordered a new (style, style of) wall decoration for the office. _____
7. I was (to, at) the celebration last week. _____
8. What can we do (beside, besides) writing a letter of complaint? _____
9. I want to go along (to, too, two). _____
10. (Two, to, too) many times I hear the same complaints. _____
11. Did you (graduate, graduate from) high school? _____
12. He (too, to, two) feels that (too, to, two) hours are enough. _____
13. The shirt was almost ripped (off of, off) the crooner's back. _____
14. The idol has toppled (off of, from) its pedestal. _____
15. Is there a great difference (among, between) the Ford and the Chevrolet? _____
16. He opened the door and went (in, into) the room. _____
17. I would (of, have) been there if it had not been for the rain. _____
18. She should (have, of) been there too. _____
19. There were bees (between, among) the many flowers. _____
20. (Between, Among) the ten contestants, Consuela was chosen. _____

UNIT 14

the right preposition (1)

Introduction

Tradition and usage dictate that certain words are followed by one preposition rather than another. You will be using many of these words and their accompanying prepositions daily in your work. Therefore, it is important that you learn these expressions so that you can recall them automatically.

In this unit we will present these expressions in small groups. We will ask you to memorize them and then to use them in practice exercises.

In the past tense, the standard forms of be are: I was; he, she, or it was; we were; you were; they were. Was is the form used when the subject is singular, were when the subject is plural. At one time there was a singular form of the word you (thou), but in that period of time you, the plural form, was used in formal situations even when addressing a single person. Since the singular form of you has been dropped from the language, you are and you were continue to be used even in speaking to a single person. You is and you was are incorrect.

Memorize the following words with their correct prepositions.

abide by (a decision)
absolve from (to free from)
abstain from (usual combination)
accede to (to express approval or give consent)
accompanied by (a person)
accompanied with (an object)
according to (done according to directions)

adapted to (adjusted to)
adhere to (to give support or to hold fast)
affiliate with (to associate oneself)
agree with (an opinion)
agree to (terms)
agree among (more than two people)
agree between (two people)

Page 115

A. In the space provided, write the preposition that best completes the thought.

1. Abide _____ a referee's decision.
2. Accompanied _____ his boss.
3. Accede _____ his wishes.
4. Adapted _____ your needs.
5. Agree _____ his views on politics.
6. Agree _____ the terms of the contract.
7. Accompanied _____ a full payment.
8. According _____ our contract.
9. Abstain _____ voting.
10. Absolve _____ all guilt.
11. Adhere _____ my previous decision.
12. Agree _____ the two of us.
13. Agree _____ the three of us.
14. Affiliate _____ the law firm.

Memorize the following words with their correct prepositions.

angry with (a person)
angry at (an occurrence or object)
annoyed with (a person)
annoyed by (that which annoys)
appropriate to (suitable to)
argue with (a person)
argue for (something)
attend to (heed; listen; to direct one's care)
beneficial to (not *for*)
blame for (not *on*)
borrow from (not *of*)
buy from (not *of*)
capable of (having sufficient intelligence, resources, or strength)
careless about (appearance)
careless in (performance of actions)
careless of (others)

B. In the space provided, write the preposition that best completes the thought.

1. Angry _____ the superintendent.
2. Angry _____ the rainy weather.
3. Buy _____ a salesman.
4. Borrow _____ a friend.
5. Attend _____ business.
6. Argue _____ his brother.
7. Beneficial _____ his employees.
8. Capable _____ the task.
9. Careless _____ his teammates.
10. Blame _____ the accident.
11. Careless _____ her dress.
12. Argue _____ the cause.
13. Annoyed _____ Mr. Jones.
14. Annoyed _____ the mosquito.
15. Careless _____ his work.
16. Appropriate _____ the occasion.

UNIT 14

the right preposition (2)

Memorize the following words with their correct prepositions.

cause for (an action)
cause of (a result)
choose among (three or more)
choose between (two)
compare to (suggest a similarity)
compare with (specific similarities)
complementary to (not *with*)

comply with (not *to*)
coincide with (usual combination)
concur in (an opinion)
concur with (a person or thing)
confer with (compare views or take counsel)
confide in (to tell confidentially)
confide to (to entrust)

A. In the space provided, write the preposition that best completes the thought.

1. Cause _____ alarm.
2. Choose _____ his two friends.
3. Concur _____ Mrs. Smith.
4. Concur _____ their judgment.
5. Choose _____ the three.
6. Confer _____ your doctor.
7. Confide _____ his brother.
8. Cause _____ the accident.
9. Complementary _____ each other.
10. Confide _____ his brother that . . .

Memorize the following words with their correct prepositions.

consist of (is made up of)
consist in (lies in)
contrast to (or *with* when **contrast** is a noun)
contrast with (when **contrast** is a verb)
convenient to (a location)
convenient for (a purpose)
conversant with (well informed)
correspond with (writing letters)
correspond to (equivalent)
dates from (not *back to*)

deal in (kind of business)
deal with (people)
depend upon (or *on*; to become conditioned)
differ from (a thing)
differ with (an opinion)
disappointed at (or *in* a thing)
disappointed with (a person)
disgusted with (a person)
disgusted at (a thing)
disgusted by (behavior)

Page 117

B. In the space provided, write the preposition that best completes the thought.

1. Correspond _____ my understanding.
2. Convenient _____ all business needs.
3. Correspond _____ his firm by mail.
4. Convenient _____ all trains.
5. Consist _____ wood and metal.
6. In contrast _____ other methods.
7. To contrast _____ other methods.
8. Dates _____ last June.
9. Deal _____ stocks and bonds.
10. Deal _____ a problem.
11. Conversant _____ the rules.
12. Disappointed _____ John.
13. Depend _____ his parents.
14. Differs _____ our old desk.
15. Differs _____ his boss.
16. Disappointed _____ the outcome.
17. Disgusted _____ his boss.
18. Disgusted _____ the sight.
19. Disgusted _____ his actions.
20. Consist _____ the truth.

Memorize the following words with their correct prepositions.

dispense with (not *of*)
dissent from (not *with* or *of*)
emerge from (to arise from)
enter into (inquire into or become a part of)
enter upon (a career)
entertained by (amused, diverted)
equivalent to (equal)
equivalent with (synonymous)

familiar with (conversant)
in accordance with (not *to*)
in compliance with (usual combination)
identical with (uniform with)
identical to (equal to)
impose upon (or *on* meaning to infringe or abuse)

C. In the space provided, write the preposition that best completes the thought.

1. Familiar _____ the entire process.
2. In accordance _____ the vast majority.
3. Emerge _____ the depths of despair.
4. Equivalent _____ a full gallon.
5. Entertained _____ the comedian.
6. Impose _____ your neighbors.
7. Enter _____ an agreement.
8. Dispense _____ the minutes.
9. Dissent _____ the group.
10. Enter _____ a secretarial career.
11. Equivalent _____ your thoughts.
12. Identical _____ your proposal.
13. Identical _____ that sum.
14. In compliance _____ your order.

UNIT 14

the right preposition (3)

Memorize the following words with their correct prepositions.

coincide with (agree with)
compare to (suggest a similarity)
compare with (specific similarities)
comply with (not *to*)
necessity for (urgent need)
necessity of (unavoidable obligation)

need for (urgent occasion for)
need of (lack or want)
object to (to oppose)
offended at (action)
offended with (a person)
participate in (to take part)

A. In the space provided, write the preposition that best completes the thought.

1. Need _____ your presence.
2. Need _____ a blanket.
3. Object _____ certain conditions.
4. Participate _____ a contest.
5. Comply _____ your request.
6. Coincide _____ the plans of others.
7. Offended _____ your remark.
8. Offended _____ his boss.
9. Necessity _____ a doctor.
10. Necessity _____ my presence.
11. Compare this _____ that.
12. Compared _____ the larger one . . .

Memorize the following words with their correct prepositions.

payment for (an article)
payment of (a fee or bill)
proceed with (to continue)
proceed from (to come forth)
profit by (not *from*)

prohibit from (is usual form)
provide for (to supply what is needed)
take exception to (usual combination)
talk to (to speak to a person)

B. In the space provided, write the preposition that best completes the thought.

1. Payment _____ the chair.
2. Proceed _____ the story.
3. Profit _____ your mistakes.
4. Prohibit _____ entering here.
5. Provide _____ your children.
6. Take exception _____ that statement.
7. Talk _____ your mother.
8. Proceed _____ the back of the room.
9. Payment _____ the doctor's fees.

Page 119

If you want to know whether a word is suitable for writing or speaking in a formal situation, you can find out from your dictionary. Words that are *nonstandard* are so noted in some dictionaries; in others, they are called *colloquial, dialectal,* or *slang*. (Such terms are usually abbreviated.) In some formal situations, you will want to avoid all such words, as well as the ones followed by the words *vulgar* or *usually considered vulgar*.

Review

A. Using the following list, select the missing preposition for each sentence and write that preposition in the space provided. It may be necessary to use the same preposition in more than one sentence.

about	at	from	of
among	between	in	to
around	during	into	with

1. This solution may differ _____ the one you had in mind.
2. Your idea is different _____ the one I had.
3. _____ you and me, I prefer to shop at that store.
4. I will place your painting _____ my many treasures.
5. She differs _____ your decision.
6. The boy went _____ the house.
7. The boy is _____ the kitchen.
8. She was graduated _____ high school last June.
9. I was _____ her birthday party.
10. The executive committee met _____ the weekend.
11. They will meet _____ my home tonight.
12. Go _____ the hospital at once.
13. He will arrive _____ an hour from now.
14. He went _____ the corner to visit a friend.
15. What type _____ position do you hold?

UNIT 14
the right preposition (4)

assignment

A. The first half of a letter appears on this page, and the concluding half on page 122. The letter contains a number of errors in the use of prepositions. Cross out each error and make the correction above it.

Dear Mr. Smith:

I am afraid that I cannot agree upon your interpretation of our contract. Your interpretation is entirely different than mine. Unfortunately, my attorney, accompanied with his family, is at a vacation so that I have been unable to obtain his advice. I am trying to correspond to him by mail, but up until today have been unable to locate him.

This difference of opinion among you and me must be reconciled at once. You realize that I am not angry at you. I am angry at the conditions that brought about this situation.

B. The following is the continuation of the letter begun on page 121. Cross out each error and make the correction above it.

I am quite willing to comply to all the provisions in Paragraph X, but I cannot agree to your interpretation of Paragraph XI. When I agreed to enter in this contract, I interpreted Paragraph XI very differently than your present interpretation.

Was it merely convenient to you to change your mind once I was bound by the contract? You cannot be indifferent to standard business practice, and my understanding to the contract is in complete accord with standard business usage. Paragraph XI is identical to Paragraph VII of the Standard Business Contract No. 109.

I am forwarding a copy of this letter, accompanied by a copy of Paragraph XI, up to the National Business Board.

I will abide with their decision if you will agree to abide with it too.

Respectfully,

If English is not your native language, the extra effort of listening to radio and television programs in English rather than your native language will pay off in improving your pronunciation. Notice the rhythm as well as the pronunciation of words when English is spoken by people whose profession involves speaking.

UNIT 15
choosing pronouns (1)

Introduction

In Unit 5 you learned that pronouns take different forms, depending upon how they are used in a sentence. In this unit we will talk further about pronouns and give you guidelines for choosing the correct pronoun for any given sentence.

The different forms a pronoun can take are called *cases*. There are three cases of pronouns: the *nominative case,* the *objective case,* and the *possessive case*. The use the pronoun has in a particular sentence will dictate which case to use.

Here are the nominative pronouns:

	Singular	*Plural*
First Person:	I	we
Second Person:	you	you
Third Person:	he, she, it	they

Who is a nominative pronoun; it is both singular and plural.

The nominative case of the pronoun is used as the *subject* of a sentence or of a clause:

    I want to go.   **They** want to see the movie.

The nominative case is used after a *linking verb:*

    It is **he.**   It is **we.**

Here are the objective pronouns:

	Singular	*Plural*
First Person:	me	us
Second Person:	you	you
Third Person:	him, her, it	them

Whom is an objective pronoun; it is both singular and plural.

The objective case of the pronoun is used as the *object of a verb* or the *object of a preposition:*

Page 123

He thanked **me.** (*Me* is the object of the verb *thanked.*)
Give it to **me.** (*Me* is the object of the preposition *to.*)

You studied the possessive pronouns in Unit 5 and will find the list of possessive pronouns on page 39. Note also that *whose* is a possessive pronoun; it is both singular and plural.

A. Fill in the missing pronouns in the following chart.

	Nominative Case		*Objective Case*		*Possessive Case*	
	Singular	*Plural*	*Singular*	*Plural*	*Singular*	*Plural*
First Person	I		me			our
Second Person		you				
					yours	
Third Person	he			them		
			it			

B. In the space provided, write the correct pronoun.

1. (I, Me) am extremely pleased with his progress. _____
2. (He, Him) is an exceptionally gifted salesman. _____
3. Last night (us, we) went to the theater after dinner. _____
4. In the long run (her, she) will undoubtedly succeed. _____
5. Contrary to our advice (them, they) all agreed to the resolution. _____

Just as there is standard English, there are standard business manners, neither better nor worse than others, but simply standard. Observe successful people's manners and practice them. In some cultures, for example, it is not polite to look a superior directly in the eye. In our country standard manners require that one *does* look directly in the eye of the person to whom one is speaking. Don't stare steadily, however, for that is not standard in the United States.

Page 124   choosing pronouns (1)

UNIT 15

choosing pronouns (2)

Us and **we:** Sometimes the structure of a sentence makes it difficult to decide on the correct pronoun. The pronouns *us* and *we* can be misused easily in sentences where the subject or the object is hard to locate. Look at this sentence:

We secretaries have interesting work.

The word *secretaries* makes the sentence somewhat tricky. If you leave out *secretaries* you can see that the nominative pronoun *we,* rather than the objective pronoun *us,* should be used.

Here is another example:

The prize was given to **us** girls.

If you read the sentence to yourself without the word *girls* you can see that *us* is the object of the preposition *to* and must be in the objective case.

A. In the space provided, write the correct word.

1. The director asked (us, we) boys to be present. _____
2. (Us, We) students should be cheerful and efficient. _____
3. Mr. Jones gave the production award to (us, we) secretaries. _____
4. The meal pleased (us, we) ladies very much. _____
5. (Us, We) typists should study some kind of shorthand. _____

Than and **as:** To choose the proper pronoun after *than* or *as* add a word that completes the meaning of the sentence—a word such as *am, do, for,* or *was.*

She is a better stenographer than **I.**

By adding *am* after the pronoun you can see that the nominative form is correct. (Using *me* after the word *than* would be incorrect in this sentence.) The pronoun *I* is the subject of the understood verb *am*.

                She was not so good as **he.**

The sentence means: *She was not so good as* **he was.** (Using *him* after the word *as* would be incorrect in this sentence.) The pronoun *he* is the subject of the understood verb *was*.

A. In the space provided, write the correct word.

1. Frank is more ambitious than (her, she). _____
2. He would rather work for Mr. Clark than (me, I). _____
3. She does a better job than (I, me). _____
4. He would rather eat with John than (me, I). _____
5. He was not ready as soon as (she, her). _____

B. In the space provided, write the correct pronoun to be used after each linking verb.

1. It is (I, me). _____
2. It is (he, him). _____
3. It is (them, they). _____
4. It was (I, me). _____
5. It was (us, we). _____

C. Underline the correct pronoun for each sentence below.

1. They hired (I, me) for the job.
2. They hired (he, him) for the job.
3. The decision shocked (he, him).
4. The explosion knocked (her, she) out of her chair.
5. In the end he lent (us, we) his support.
6. Send (them, they) the letters at once.
7. Permit (I, me) to voice my disapproval.
8. You have told (us, we) a most fascinating story.
9. They would not allow (he, him) to leave.
10. The director told (us, we) that his decision had been reached.

    Standard manners require that people standing and talking be separated by two to three feet. If you come from a culture in which people stand closer, try to practice the two-to-three-foot "standing distance."

UNIT 15

choosing pronouns (3)

Joining Proper Pronouns

Use the same form of a pronoun when it is joined with another pronoun or a noun that you would use if the pronoun were alone.

>The invoice was sent by **him** and **me.**

Both pronouns in the sentence above are in the objective case; they are both objects of the preposition *by*.

>**He** and **I** are experts.

Both pronouns in this sentence are in the nominative case; they are both subjects of the sentence.

>Did you know it was Bob and **he?**

Because the pronoun follows a linking verb, it is in the nominative case.

A. Write the correct pronoun in the space provided.

1. Bob and (he, him) will go. _____
2. The men congratulated Mr. Robinson and (I, me). _____
3. Mr. Smith will introduce you and (he, him) to the staff. _____
4. Our office is certain that you and (her, she) will get the job. _____
5. (He, Him) and (I, me) will leave on the early train. _____
6. They gave raises in salary to (he, him) and (I, me). _____
7. The winners of the prizes were (he, him) and (her, she). _____
8. Between you and (I, me), this is a dangerous proposition. _____
9. The salesmen in your territory are Mr. Johnson and (I, me). _____
10. The boys and (I, me) feel certain that the contract will be awarded to you and (they, them). _____

Between you and me: In Unit 13 you learned that *between* is a preposition. In the phrase *between you and me* you can see that *me* is the object of the preposition *between*. It would never be correct to use the nominative pronoun *I* to complete this phrase.

>**Between you and me,** I think this will work.

The objective case should follow *between* in sentences such as the following:

The profits were divided **between** Mrs. Smith and **him.**

A. Write the correct pronoun in the space provided.

1. Between you and (I, me), who do you think will win? _____
2. The boss divided the work between (he, him) and (me, I). _____
3. The cake was divided evenly between Joan and (she, her). _____
4. Between you and (I, me), did you like the play? _____
5. Mr. Jones divided the books between Susan and (he, him). _____

Review

A. In the space provided, write the correct preposition for each sentence.

1. The employees agreed (with, to) the terms of the contract. _____
2. The child was accompanied (by, with) her mother. _____
3. The young man plans to affiliate (to, with) a small law firm. _____
4. As a driver, he is careless (about, of) others. _____
5. They placed the blame (on, for) the mishap on John. _____
6. The manager has agreed to comply (to, with) your request. _____
7. She was disgusted (by, at) his behavior. _____
8. Mr. Smith knows how to deal (with, in) his customers skillfully. _____
9. The sculpture consists (in, of) metal and wood. _____
10. Your feelings correspond (to, with) mine on this matter. _____
11. He lives (on, at) 9 Maple Avenue. _____
12. Please do not interfere (at, with) me. _____
13. Here is the payment (of, for) the furniture I purchased. _____
14. I believe he should abide (by, in) the rules. _____
15. He is capable (of, for) doing better work. _____
16. She is angry (with, at) her sister. _____
17. He gave it to (he, him) and me. _____
18. It was (he and I, him and me) that you saw at the racetrack. _____
19. Please do not be angry (with, at) me. _____
20. Charlotte and (I, me) are coming to the party. _____

Spelling hints: Don't leave out the *-al-* in inciden*tal*ly.

UNIT 15
choosing pronouns (4)

assignment

A. In the space provided, write the correct pronoun.

1. Give it to (he, him). _____
2. (He, Him) likes this method of accounting. _____
3. This will shock (he, him). _____
4. It was (he, him) who started the trouble. _____
5. This message is for (she, her). _____
6. Here is a story that will astound (they, them). _____
7. Was it (I, me) you saw at the theater? _____
8. Are you sure you sent (I, me) the bill? _____
9. John and (he, him) are next on the list. _____
10. Give the order to Charles and (he, him). _____
11. (We, Us) salesmen must plan our campaign carefully. _____
12. (He and I) (Him and me) will leave at dawn. _____
13. Was it (he, him) you spoke to? _____
14. The order directed (us, we) secretaries to come to work fifteen minutes earlier. _____
15. He is not so clever as (I, me). _____

> **Memorize the spelling of these words: *supersede, exceed, proceed,* and *succeed.* All other words that have the same sound in the final syllable as theirs spell that syllable *cede* (*secede*).**

B. In the space provided, write the correct pronoun.

1. This man is a better salesman than (I, me). _____
2. He would rather work with John than (I, me). _____
3. Between you and (I, me), this work is easy. _____
4. Mr. Roberts is as good a manager as (he, him). _____
5. It was (she, her) who cut the endowment fund. _____
6. The trophy was presented to Smith and (I, me). _____
7. He is pleased with (their, they're) success. _____
8. Is Judith taller than (she, her)? _____
9. They would rather choose Robert than (I, me). _____
10. It is up to (us, we) girls to show her the proper procedure. _____
11. The letter was sent directly to (he, him). _____
12. We knew that (she, her) would accept the offer. _____
13. It was (I, me) who ordered the books from (they, them). _____
14. Did you see (us, we) at the theater? _____
15. If I were (her, she), I would demand a raise. _____

UNIT 16

more about pronouns (1)

Introduction

The pronouns *who* and *whom* sometimes cause trouble. You should remember that *who* is in the nominative case, while *whom* is in the objective case.

Since *who* is in the nominative case, it may be used in only two situations: as the subject of a sentence or clause and after a linking verb.

Who threw the ball?   It is **who?**

Whom should be used as the object of a verb or the object of a preposition.

Whom do you want?   You are referring to **whom?**

If you have trouble choosing between *who* and *whom* for a particular sentence, substitute *he* or *him*. If *he* fits, *who* is correct; if *him* fits, *whom* is correct. For example:

I wonder **whom** we should give the prize to.

You may substitute the pronoun *him* and say:

We should give the prize to **him.**

Look at this sentence:

He is the man **who** I believe erased the signature.

By substituting *he,* you could rearrange the clause to read:

I believe **he** erased the signature.

Additionally, there is sometimes confusion about whether to write the pronouns *anyone, someone,* or *everyone* as one word or two. Remember to write any of these pronouns as one word unless it is followed by a phrase beginning with *of.* In that case, write it as two words.

Page 131

Everyone is present.
Every one of the men was present.

No one is always written as two words.

No one is here today.

A. In the space provided, write the correct pronoun.

1. (Who, Whom) is it? _____
2. He is a man (who, whom) is loved by all. _____
3. He is a man (who, whom) we all love. _____
4. There is an urgent need for men (who, whom) we can trust. _____
5. He is a man (who, whom) I am positive can be trusted. _____
6. (Who, Whom) did you say was at the door? _____
7. The man (who, whom) I think will be our next president will be here soon. _____
8. The man (who, whom) I believe we all love is standing next to me. _____
9. (Who, Whom) in your opinion will win the game? _____
10. I wonder (whom, who) we will see there. _____

B. In the space provided, write the correct word or words.

1. Can (any one, anyone) enter the contest? _____
2. Let (any one, anyone) of the members enter. _____
3. (Every one, Everyone) of the girls may go. _____
4. (No one, Noone) has gone yet. _____
5. (Some one, Someone) is at the door. _____

The way you pronounce words will influence a prospective employer's attitude toward you. Self-confident people speak clearly; people who are unsure of themselves tend to mumble.

UNIT 16

more about pronouns (2)

Whoever and **whomever**: *Whoever* is in the nominative case. *Whomever* is in the objective case. In choosing between the two pronouns, you can substitute *he* for *whoever,* and *him* for *whomever* in the sentence in question. When you do this, disregard all words in the sentence before *whoever* or *whomever*.

   Give the prize to **whoever** deserves it.

In this sentence disregard *Give the prize to;* the phrase **he** *deserves it* will make sense. Therefore, the nominative pronoun *whoever* is correct.

A. In the space provided, write the correct pronoun.

1. (Whoever, Whomever) answers the phone should be pleasant. _____
2. Give the prize to (whoever, whomever) you please. _____
3. She always accepts help from (whoever, whomever) will give it. _____
4. I will choose (whoever, whomever) is better. _____
5. I will choose (whoever, whomever) I wish. _____
6. The dog will bark at (whoever, whomever) comes here. _____
7. She will choose (whoever, whomever) she likes best. _____
8. (Whoever, Whomever) arrives late will regret it. _____
9. He will give assistance to (whoever, whomever) asks for it. _____
10. (Whoever, Whomever) drives the car should be careful. _____

Whose and **who's**: *Whose* is a possessive pronoun. *Who's* is the contraction of the two words *who is.* Although *whose* and *who's*

Page 133

sound the same, it is important to use the correct form in your written work.

> **Whose** book is lost?
> **Who's** going to the luncheon?

A. In the space provided, write the correct word.

1. I don't know (who's, whose) pen I have. _____
2. Tell me (who's, whose) dictation this is. _____
3. I'll tell you (who's, whose) responsible for this confusion. _____
4. (Who's, Whose) coming for dinner tonight? _____
5. (Who's, Whose) coat is on the chair? _____

B. In the space provided, write the correct word.

1. (Who, Whom) is at the door? _____
2. It is (who, whom) that you want to meet? _____
3. (Who, Whom) did you say called? _____
4. Our choice is a man (who, whom) you all know. _____
5. Our choice is a man (who, whom) is known by all. _____
6. He likes (whoever, whomever) is kind to him. _____
7. He is a man (who, whom) I think can be fully trusted in his position. _____
8. (Who, Whom) were you speaking of? _____
9. (Who, Whom) among you knows the answer? _____
10. (Whomever, Whoever) gets there first wins the prize. _____
11. He likes (whoever, whomever) he meets. _____
12. She is a woman (who, whom) I feel confident we can rely on. _____
13. Upon (who, whom) will you bestow the award? _____
14. She is a person (who, whom) is most talented. _____
15. She is a person (who, whom) we know to be talented. _____

more about pronouns (2)

UNIT 16

more about pronouns (3)

Like as a preposition: When *like* is used as a preposition (meaning *similar to*), it takes the objective case of the pronoun after it.

  She swims like **me.**

A. In the space provided, write the correct pronoun.

1. He writes like (I, me). _____
2. Mary looks like (she, her). _____
3. This group performs like (they, them). _____
4. She works like (he, him) under pressure. _____
5. They play tennis like (we, us). _____

But meaning "except": Sometimes the word *but* is used as a preposition meaning *except*. The pronoun following *but* should be in the objective case.

  All but **him** are welcome.

A. In the space provided, write the correct pronoun.

1. I want anybody but (he, him) for the position. _____
2. Everyone but (she, her) went along. _____
3. No one but (I, me) may have the key. _____
4. All but (they, them) are coming. _____
5. She invited everyone but (we, us). _____
6. Every one of the men but (he, him) is here. _____

Page 135

7. Any one of the group but (she, her) could play the piano. _____

8. They want anybody but (I, me) to make the trip. _____

9. Let anyone but John and (she, her) borrow the car. _____

10. No one is here but (I, me). _____

Review

A. In the space provided, write the correct pronoun.

1. If it was (he, him) who sent the order, (he, him) should be congratulated. _____
2. The last person to leave was (her, she). _____
3. During our last convention (we, us) presented the idea. _____
4. Until now (he, him) has the best selling record. _____
5. The professor told (us, we) that the exam will be Friday. _____
6. The correspondence was sent by (her, she). _____
7. The package was addressed to (me, I). _____
8. The notice instructed (us, we) employees to remain for a meeting today. _____
9. Her brother and (her, she) will arrive at noon. _____
10. The party will be a surprise to (they, them). _____
11. She gave the boxes to Mrs. Smith and (she, her). _____
12. She paints better than (he, him). _____
13. I am as happy as (her, she). _____
14. Could it have been (us, we) who swayed his opinion? _____
15. To preserve our position as leader in our field, (me, I) propose a new concept. _____

Do not confuse clear speech with loud speech. Speak only loudly enough to be heard by the person you are addressing.

name   section   date

UNIT 16

more about pronouns (4)

assignment

A. A number of pronouns in the following letter are misused. Cross out each incorrect pronoun and write the correct pronoun above it.

Dear Mr. Backrack:

I would like to tell you more about Robert Gilbert, the man who I started to describe to you last week. Mr. Gilbert is a man who has been constantly employed in top executive positions. Ten years ago it was him and Bob Anthony whom raised the Eighth National Bank to its present position. It was him whom gave the Smith Company it's shot in the arm. It was him whom the Jones Corporation called upon when it needed help.

There are few such men left in the business world. If it were left to I, I would definitely choose Robert Gilbert for the Presidency of this firm. He is a man whom I believe can lead us out of our present difficulty. He is a man whom I believe we can accept as a leader and an inspiration. He is a man whom I believe will lead us to the top position in our field.

I am sure that whoever the Board chooses as President will do a fine job; however, I would choose Robert Gilbert. I cannot think of a man whom is better qualified, whom is more trustworthy, and whom will do a better job than him. If it were up to we salesmen, we would choose noone but he as a man whose reliable.

              Respectfully,

B. Cross out any incorrect words in the following sentences and write the correct word on the line provided. There may be more than one error in a sentence.

1. Tell me whose coming today so that no one but he will be expected. _____
2. Everyone of the officials except he has been assigned a post. _____
3. Who's typewriter needs repairing, his or your's? _____
4. There's would be a most difficult task for any one. _____
5. There roles would be exciting for any one with courage. _____
6. Every one wishes they could sing like he. _____
7. Between you and I, no one is sure of his part. _____
8. The salesman whose coming looks like him. _____
9. Our's is a perfect relationship, and every one knows it. _____
10. Your's is not so accurate as our's. _____
11. If that's him at the door now, tell him that every one is waiting. _____
12. The secret is between you and he, so don't tell anyone of your friends. _____
13. All but her are here; show everyone the report. _____
14. I don't know who's book is on the chair next to they. _____
15. Whose going to visit the museum with she and me? _____

UNIT 17
conjunctions (1)

Introduction

A *conjunction* is a part of speech that joins ideas. *And, but, because, or,* and *yet* are just a few of the hundreds of conjunctions in our language.

> We purchased stock **and** then we sold it.

In addition to connecting two or more ideas, conjunctions show the relationship between ideas. Being able to select the conjunction which *best* connects your ideas will benefit you in both speaking and writing. For example:

> This book is heavy to carry, **but** it is light reading.

There are two ideas in this sentence: *the book is heavy* and *the reading is light*. The conjunction *but* is more appropriate than *and* in this case, since *but* points up the contrast between the *heavy book* and the *light reading*.

Types of Sentences

To use conjunctions skillfully you must keep in mind the three types of sentences: *simple, compound,* and *complex*. Conjunctions are used to connect clauses of both compound and complex sentences.

A compound sentence is composed of two or more clauses of equal rank that are joined together by a conjunction or a semicolon. In a compound sentence, the conjunction that connects one clause with another is called a *coordinate conjunction*. The coordinate conjunctions include *and, but, or, nor, for,* and sometimes *so* and *yet*.

> The snow fell **and** the sleet froze.

The two independent clauses are *the snow fell* and *the sleet froze*. Each clause could stand alone as a sentence.

A complex sentence is composed of an independent clause

and a dependent clause. A conjunction that introduces the dependent clause is called a *subordinate conjunction* because it makes that clause incomplete by itself. Subordinate conjunctions include *because, unless, after, if, since, otherwise, until,* and *while.*

>We selected their product **because** it is best.

Because is the subordinate conjunction. The dependent clause is *because it is best;* it leaves you up in the air without expressing a complete thought. The independent clause is *We selected their product;* it expresses a complete thought.

Conjunctions and Prepositions

Words like *before, after,* and *but* may serve either as conjunctions or prepositions depending on the sentence in question. As conjunctions they are followed by the nominative case of the pronoun; as prepositions they are followed by the objective case.

>I got to the office **after him.** (preposition)
>I got to the office **after he** did. (conjunction)

A. In the space provided, write each independent clause.

EXAMPLE: When the patents expire, this plant will close.   this plant will close.

1. Since we went away, time has flown.
2. Forgetting his manners, he remained seated.
3. We won't forget this if we live to be a hundred.
4. They came; they saw; they conquered.
5. I feel satisfied.
6. Mail a check for the balance as soon as possible.
7. They tried to resist, but they could not.
8. Either they go or we do.
9. Although he is on in years, he is sprightly.
10. Won't you come in without further delay?

UNIT 17

conjunctions (2)

Types of Sentences

In a complex sentence, the *natural sequence* is for the independent clause to precede the dependent clause.

> **We shall pay the bill** unless we hear from you.

You can reverse the sentence if you like.

> Unless we hear from you, **we shall pay the bill.**

When you put the dependent clause first, as in the sentence above, you use a comma to separate the clauses.

A. In the space provided, mark *N* if the sentence follows the natural sequence and mark *U* if the sequence is in unnatural order. Insert a comma in any sentence from which it is omitted.

1. As soon as we arrived the festivities began. _____
2. Assuming that he was right he proceeded without further instructions. _____
3. We will order now although we are overstocked. _____
4. Until I hear from you I shall say no more. _____
5. We won't despair while there is still hope. _____
6. Although he is still a minor he is old enough to be responsible. _____
7. Because he was modest he refused adulation. _____
8. We will fight back until they retreat. _____
9. Don't underestimate the opposition if you hope to conquer them. _____
10. Before I leave let me congratulate you. _____

B. In the space provided, indicate what type of sentence each is—either simple, compound, or complex.

1. Since we went away, time has flown. _____
2. Forgetting his manners, he remained seated. _____

3. We won't forget this if we live to be a hundred. _____

4. They came; they saw; they conquered. _____

5. I feel satisfied. _____

An interjection is a word or group of words that expresses strong feeling. You use interjections in your everyday conversation. When you use an interjection in writing remember that it is followed by an exclamation point. Good! Well done! Oh! Surprise!

Correlative Conjunctions

Certain conjunctions act together to connect ideas. They are called *correlative conjunctions* because they correlate one thought with another.

either . . . or: **Either** you work harder **or** you leave.
neither . . . nor: We want **neither** sympathy **nor** charity.
both . . . and: The true leader is **both** self-confident **and** humble.
not only . . . but also: We want you **not only** to visit our office **but also** to inspect our plant.
whether . . . or: **Whether** you act now **or** wait is a matter of great concern.

These correlative conjunctions should be used in the pairs indicated. With *neither* always use *nor*, rather than *or*. Likewise, *either* and *or* should be used together.

Correlative conjunctions should stand as near as possible to the words they connect:

My job has given me **both** pleasure **and** satisfaction.

A. In the space provided, write the correct word.

1. Either you ship the goods (or, and) I will sue. _____
2. Neither the chair (or, nor) the desk is in perfect condition. _____
3. Both the fan (and, or) the motor were defective. _____
4. He not only refused to accept the goods (but, but also) refused to pay. _____
5. Neither the dictionary (or, nor) the glossary included the term. _____
6. He not only gave us dinner (but, but also) invited us to stay for the evening. _____
7. They are willing to offer you not only a discount (but, but also) a bonus gift. _____
8. They offered either a straight salary (and, or) a commission. _____
9. Our latest model is not only functional (but, but also) artistic. _____
10. Either the ledger (or, nor) the receipt is incorrect. _____

UNIT 17
conjunctions (3)

Choosing Conjunctions

There are several conjunctions which require special attention.

As: The preposition *like* is often misused for the conjunction *as*. This sentence is wrong:

> **Like** I said, this is a great day.

As is used correctly in these sentences:

> It was done **as** you wanted.
> He dictates **as** I do.

Provided: *Provided* is a conjunction. *Providing* is not a conjunction and should never be used to join two parts of a sentence.

> We will arrive on time **provided** we have a tailwind.

So: *So* is a conjunction that is used more frequently than it should be. It is better to use words like *therefore, consequently,* and *accordingly* to join ideas. These words enable you to express your ideas more precisely than you can by using *so*.

So . . . as: When two *affirmative* statements are joined by paired conjunctions, use *as . . . as;* when *negative* statements are joined, use *so . . . as*.

> He is **as** tall **as** a tree.
> He is not **so** tall **as** I had thought.

Where: Be careful not to use the conjunction *where* when you really mean *that*. This sentence is correct:

> I read in the magazine **that** the price had been lowered.

That: It is not correct to say *the reason was because*. The conjunction *that* should be used in place of *because*:

> The reason was **that** I was tired.

And: To use *and* after *try* in this sentence is not correct:

> You must try **and** do it.

The sentence should be:

> You must try **to** do it.

Page 143

A. In the space provided, write the correct word.

1. I acted (as, like) you advised. _____
2. Would you try (and, to) correct the error. _____
3. We will accept (provided, providing) you lower your price. _____
4. We would appreciate it if you would try (and, to) locate the lost files. _____
5. The computer was fully (as, so) large as a room. _____
6. We will go not only to Paris (but, but also) to London. _____
7. This contract is valid (provided, providing) the shipment arrives on schedule. _____
8. (Like, As) I said yesterday, this must stop. _____
9. Neither time (or, nor) effort is to be spared (provided, providing) they cooperate. _____
10. It looks very much (like, as) your automatic washer. _____
11. He is here (like, as) we requested. _____
12. She did the report (like, as) they wanted. _____
13. They will come (providing, provided) it does not rain. _____
14. She is not (as, so) efficient as we had thought. _____
15. The reason was (because, that) she was sick. _____

Review

A. In the space provided, write the correct pronoun.

1. I believe he is the man (whom, who) can do the job. _____
2. You may invite (anyone, any one) you wish. _____
3. Mary writes neatly like (he, him). _____
4. (Everyone, Every one) of the athletes is here. _____
5. (Who, Whom) will you take to the airport? _____
6. Give the tickets to (whoever, whomever) pays you first. _____
7. He will give a book to all but (she, her). _____
8. Do you know (whose, who's) knocking at the door? _____
9. Do you know (whose, who's) car is in the driveway? _____
10. No one but (us, we) is here yet. _____

name   section   date

UNIT 17

conjunctions (4)

assignment

A. There are errors concerning conjunctions in the following sentences. Cross out the incorrect conjunctions. In the space provided, write the correct conjunction.

1. He is not as smart as I thought he was. _____
2. I read in a book where censorship is on the increase. _____
3. The reason I left was because I was tired. _____
4. The reason he was discharged was because he had been late too often. _____
5. Acme Products is not as large as General Electric. _____
6. The gain is not as great as I had anticipated. _____
7. I notice in the newspapers where employment figures are increasing. _____
8. I read where China and Russia are feuding. _____
9. I heard where Frank was promoted in his firm. _____
10. This looks excellent like I expected. _____
11. I will try and go to the store this afternoon. _____
12. She did the typing like you wanted. _____
13. Neither John or Tom were here today. _____
14. We want him not only to mow the grass but to prune the trees. _____
15. Whether he leaves today and waits is still to be decided. _____

B. In the following copy, cross out all errors and write your corrections in the space above. Insert any omitted punctuation.

Like I said in my last letter, sales have not only fallen but we have lost some salesmen too. This is not as bad as you might think since we were going to try and hire some new salesmen anyway. You probably have read in the papers where the reason sales are down is because demand has fallen. Providing this downward trend in demand is reversed I feel confident our sales will soon be back to record levels.

C. There are errors concerning conjunctions in the following sentences. Cross out the incorrect conjunctions. In the space provided, write the correct conjunction.

1. I expect our meeting will be both informative but profitable. _____
2. I want to interrupt neither your employees or your routine. _____
3. My employer has neither studied in high school nor in college. _____
4. He is so rich as Midas. _____
5. He is not as strong as Hercules. _____
6. I read in the WALL STREET JOURNAL where stock prices are advancing. _____
7. The tax penalty will not be as high as before providing that forms are filed on time. ____
8. Please try and finish by five o'clock. _____
9. Since he is arriving late we will eat dinner first. _____
10. The reason he arrived late is because the weather was bad. _____

UNIT 18

common errors (1)

Introduction

In this unit many common errors in usage will be discussed. Most of the errors concern either the addition of unnecessary words or the confusion of one word with another similar word.

You have studied some of these problem areas in previous units. They are included here for emphasis.

Common words with unusual spellings (*cough, debt*) must be memorized, but most words need not be memorized. Pronounce them carefully and you will spell correctly by associating letters with sounds. Learn to recognize prefixes, roots, and suffixes because a few of them make up a great many words and if you have mastered their spellings you can apply them to words that are unfamiliar to you.

Double Subject

A pronoun is a word which is used instead of a noun. In a simple sentence it should not be used in addition to the noun. This sentence illustrates the incorrect use of the pronoun, for the subject is repeated unnecessarily:

> Mr. Smith, our President, **he** will attend the meeting.

The pronoun *he* should be omitted:

> Mr. Smith, our President, will attend the meeting.

Double Comparison

Avoid using double comparisons such as *more happier, bestest, most loveliest*. Where *er* and *est* are added to the adjective to form the comparative and superlative, it is incorrect to use *more*

Page 147

and *most* as well. Likewise, when *more* and *most* should be used, do not add *er* and *est.*

This here and **that there:** It is incorrect to say *this here book* or *that there desk.* The words *here* and *there* should be omitted:

>**This** book is interesting.
>**That** desk is beautiful.

Kind of: Never use *a* after *kind of, sort of,* or *type of.*

>This is the **type of** job I like to see.

Has got: Do not use *has got* to indicate possession.

>He **has** a fine car.

A. Each of the following sentences contains an unnecessary word or words. Cross out all unnecessary words and all improper punctuation.

1. The Ajax Company, it will open its fall season campaign soon.
2. Our sales this year have been the most highest in our history.
3. This here gentleman is interested in your offer.
4. This sort of an investment should pay big dividends.
5. Mr. Smith has got a slight cold.
6. Bob, walking down the street, he fell.
7. This sample of lace is more finer than the last one you sent.
8. That there desk would fit perfectly.
9. What type of a man is he?
10. What has he got in mind?
11. Miss Jones, our representative, she will call on you soon.
12. Undoubtedly, this is the most best model we have ever put on the market.
13. Those there machines will be the answer to your needs.
14. This kind of a job will be fine.
15. He has not got a good reason for his absence.

UNIT 18
common errors (2)

Using the Correct Word

Teach and **learn:** To *teach* means to *give* knowledge to someone else; to *learn* means to *receive* knowledge from someone or something.

      The teacher **teaches** her class.
      The class **learns** from the teacher.

Lend and **borrow:** To *lend* means to *give* someone else your property temporarily; to *borrow* means to *accept* someone else's property temporarily.

      I **lent** John my book.
      I **borrowed** John's book last week.

Loan is a noun; *lend* is a verb.

      I need a **loan** of $500.   I will **lend** it to you.

Stayed and **stood:** *Stayed* is the past tense of *stay (remain); stood* is the past tense of *stand*.

      I should have **stayed** in bed.
      The soldier **stood** at attention.

Can and **may:** *Can* means *capable of;* it refers to physical ability. *May* means *has permission to;* it refers to consent.

      Can he swim that far?
      May we have the car tonight?

Two, too, and **to:** *Two* is a number; 2. *To* is a preposition. *To* is also part of the infinitive, such as *to drive*. *Too* is a word that intensifies the meaning of something; it means *more than* or *also*.

      Send me **two** pairs of shoes.
      He rose **to** his feet.
      I want **to** go at once.
      There is **too** much work.

A. In the space provided, write the correct word.

1. When students do not like a teacher, she will find it difficult to (teach, learn) them.
_____

2. I had to (borrow, lend) money from my employer to get home. _____
3. I (stood, stayed) at the office until well after dark. _____
4. (Can, May) you reach the shelf if you stretch? _____
5. There are (to, too, two) many people in the office force. _____
6. A student who studies hard has no difficulty (learning, teaching) his lessons. _____
7. I am sure you will repay this (lend, loan) as soon as you have the money. _____
8. They (shoulda, should've) asked us before they (lent, borrowed) the money from the bank. _____
9. (Can, May) we be excused from the exercises? _____
10. Send the (to, too, two) packages (to, too, two) the Acme Agency. _____
11. Our bitter experience has (learned, taught) us to avoid risky deals. _____
12. The bank was very willing to (lend, loan) us the money despite the size of the (lend, loan) we were seeking. _____
13. The men (stayed, stood) at attention until the ceremony was over. _____
14. (Can, May) he attain the goals he set for himself? _____
15. (To, Too, Two) many cooks spoil the broth. _____

Being that: There is no such conjunction as *being that*. Use a conjunction like *since* or *because* when you are tempted to say *being that*.

    Because he is ill, I'll stay late.

Ain't: The word *ain't* is not good English usage. Use the correct form of the verb and *not*:

    I **am not** going.   He **isn't** going.

Nowheres, somewheres, and **anywheres:** Never add *s* to *nowhere, somewhere,* and *anywhere*.

    He could find it **nowhere.**

Regardless: *Regardless* is a word; **irregardless** is not a word.

    Regardless of the weather, we shall leave on time.

Over your house: Do not use the preposition *over* when you mean *at* or *to*.

    Let's play bridge **at** my house.
    Let's go **to** Jane's house.

UNIT 18

common errors (3)

Using the Correct Word

Let and **leave:** *Leave* (*left*) means *to go away*. It should not be confused with *let* meaning *to allow or permit*.

> Will you **leave** at once?   **Let** me work alone.

Leave me alone and *Let me alone* are both correct. The first suggests *politely* that you go away; the second is a firmer request that you stop irritating me.

Lead (verb), **Lead** (noun), **Led** (verb): Don't incorrectly substitute the present tense of the verb *to lead* (rhymes with *need*) for the past tense *led* (rhymes with *red*). The noun *lead* (pronounced like *red*) refers to the metal.

> He **led** the company in sales last week.
> He may **lead** his class in marks.
> The **lead** was mined as an ore.

Respectfully, respectably, and **respectively:** *Respectfully* means *full of respect* and is often used as the complimentary close of a business letter. *Respectably* means *in a decent fashion*. *Respectively* means *in proper sequence* or *in order*.

> **Respectfully** yours, John Smith
> He spoke **respectfully** to the minister.
> He was dressed **respectably.**
> I want Charles and James **respectively** to address the group.

Lose and **loose:** The verb *lose* (pronounced "looz") means *to suffer loss*. *Loose* (rhymes with *moose*) means *free, not close together,* when used as an adjective or an adverb. As a verb, *loose* means *to untie, to make free*.

> Did you **lose** your books?
> Pull the **loose** ends together.
> The animals are **loose.**

Anxious and **eager:** *Anxious* is an adjective meaning *perplexed, worried, concerned,* or *disturbed. Eager* means *enthusiastic*.

> I am **anxious** about his health.
> I am **eager** to see him.

A. Underline the correct word in each sentence.

1. He won't (let, leave) me finish my work.
2. John (lead, led) all the students in his class.
3. He closed the letter, "(Respectfully, Respectably, Respectively) yours."
4. The dentist worked on the (lose, loose) tooth.
5. I am (anxious, eager) to get a fresh start in my job.
6. He (let, left) the room angrily.
7. He has (lead, led) an athletic existence for years.
8. He gave a (respectful, respectable, respective) salute to the officer.
9. Whatever you do, do not (lose, loose) your head in an emergency.
10. He was (anxious, eager) about the hospital report.

Angry and **mad:** Use *angry* rather than *mad* to imply peevishness or great displeasure. *Mad* means *insane*.

> A **mad** person may be confined to an asylum.
> I am **angry** at his impertinence.

Disinterested and **uninterested:** A *disinterested* person is impartial, fair, interested, but aloof. An *uninterested* person is not interested.

> I want a **disinterested** arbiter.
> I am **uninterested** in the book.

Myself: Do not use *myself* when a simple pronoun is required. Pronouns ending in *self* are reflexive—the action comes back to the doer.

> I hurt **myself**.   Frank and **I** went to the movies.

And or **but** as sentence openers: *And* and *but* are coordinate conjunctions and are used to join equal words, phrases, or clauses. They should not be used to *begin* a sentence in formal writing.

> I saw Frank, **but** he didn't see me.

Then and **than:** Do not use *then,* meaning *at that time* or *later,* when you want to use the conjunction *than,* which indicates comparison.

> If you ask me, **then** I will answer. He is bigger **than** I.

B. Underline the correct word in each sentence.

1. He studies harder (than, then) she.
2. The designer liked the new colors so much, he seemed to be (mad, angry) about them.
3. A good judge must be (disinterested, uninterested) in the case before him.
4. This secret is between Frank and (me, myself).
5. Go to the office and (than, then) look for the document.

name   section   date

UNIT 18

common errors (4)

assignment

A. In the space provided, write the correct word.

1. The teacher has (taught, learned) us well. _____
2. (Loan, Lend) him your car for the evening. _____
3. Our inventory is (too, two, to) large. _____
4. (Can, May) I leave an hour early? _____
5. These stocks will maintain their value (regardless, irregardless) of the market. _____

6. If you will (leave, let) him be, he will not be so irritable. _____
7. The (lead, led) in the pencil is too soft. _____
8. That rattle seems to come from a (lose, loose) bolt in the chassis. _____
9. One should be (anxious, eager) about the effects of smoking. _____
10. The prank boomeranged and the boys hurt (them, themselves). _____

B. Cross out all unnecessary words in the following sentences.

1. Our experience shows that the Acme Company is the most best producer of farm machinery.
2. Mr. Jones he is the sort of a man you can trust.
3. This here office it is located on a residential type of a street.
4. These here salesmen, Mr. Robertson and Mr. Johnson, they have done an excellent job.
5. Did you forget to send that there message to Mr. Woodburn?

C. The following letter contains many errors. Cross out all incorrect words and phrases, and write the corrections in the space above.

Dear Mr. Abrams:

_____ Regardless of your business, you will find at the Exposition all the equipment that your office should have got. Here is your opportunity to test, to compare, and for choosing the office machinery that will fit your particular office needs.

_____ These kind of an exhibit is most unique among business shows. It is the result of the combined efforts of the exhibitors, local civic figures, the police department, and with the local business organizations.

_____ Unless your office has got all the equipment it will ever need, you and your staff should attend this important meeting. We are certain that you visiting and seeing this exposition will be an important turning point in your business career. Plan to make your ticket reservations in the very near future.

_____ Do not leave this opportunity pass, for if you loose this chance, you undoubtedly will be mad at yourself later on. We are anxious to see you at the Exposition, and we know you will not be disinterested in the equipment. We, therefore, respectively urge that you be more alert then some of your competitors. And make your reservation now.

Respectably yours,

ACME EQUIPMENT

UNIT 19
periods, question marks, and exclamation points (1)

Introduction

You have probably used the period correctly most of your life, so the five rules below will be a review for you:

1. Place a period at the end of a sentence that makes a statement. When typing a sentence, leave two spaces between the period and the first letter of the next sentence.

2. Place a period at the end of a sentence that states a command. When the command is phrased in the form of a question for the sake of politeness, use a period rather than a question mark.

> Bring it here.   Will you please bring it here.

Use the period after a condensed expression that stands for a full statement or command.

> Yes.   No.   Go.   Next.   Sit.

3. Place a period after an abbreviation.

4. Use a period to separate dollars from cents in a money amount. Do not put a period after a dollar amount if no cents are indicated.

> $2 $10 $2.00 $10.00

There is no space after the period in a dollar amount.

5. A period may be used in a numbered list such as the one you are reading now. Parentheses are also correct, but use either a period or parentheses, not both.

Basic to our way of life are these fundamental freedoms:
  1. Freedom of speech
  2. Freedom of assembly
  3. Freedom of religion
  4. Freedom of the press

Basic to our way of life are these fundamental freedoms:
  a) Freedom of speech
  b) Freedom of assembly
  c) Freedom of religion
  d) Freedom of the press

Periods

A. In the following paragraphs, circle the letters that should be capitalized. Insert all necessary periods.

(T)his morning we received a request to submit a bid on the equipment specifications for the new vocational school now being erected in Erie, Pa.

(I)t is our policy, as you know, to work only through our regular dealers. (W)e suggest, therefore, that you send a representative to follow up this opportunity for some very good business.

(W)e can be very helpful to you in preparing your estimate on the list of hand tools, and we hope you will let us work with you. (T)he large machine equipment, of course, is out of our line. (B)ecause of your long experience in this field, we know you will have no trouble in submitting a complete bid.

* * *

(W)e appreciate the information that you gave us in your letter of October 17.

(T)he purchasing agent for the Board of Education in Erie has given us permission to submit a bid on the equipment list for the new school. (S)ince the bid must be submitted on or before November 19, it is necessary for us to work rapidly.

(S)ome time ago you stated that there might be price changes after November 1. (W)hile we understand that increasing demands are being placed on the tool industry, still we must request a definite guarantee from your company that the prices in effect now will apply to the Erie school contract if it is awarded to our company.

UNIT 19

periods, question marks, and exclamation points (2)

Periods in Abbreviations

The tendency to leave periods out of abbreviations (USA, YMCA, NOW) can create a problem to which the best answer is to select a dictionary as an authority and, for the sake of consistency, use that authority. Whether your dictionary has a separate table of abbreviations or places abbreviations in the body of the dictionary, become accustomed to using the dictionary to determine whether or not to place periods after each letter. Many expressions, of course, such as *f.o.b., C. P. A.,* and so forth always use periods. Generally, abbreviations consisting of lower case letters do not have a space after the period (*i.e.; c.o.d*); since practice differs concerning leaving space when the letters are capitalized, consult your dictionary for these. People's initials, however, should have a space after each period (*J. R. Phillips*).

A. Insert periods and capital letters wherever necessary in the sentences below.

1. I will be there at eight o'clock I shall see you then
2. Step forward to volunteer that is the way to help
3. Will you open the door, please my hands are occupied
4. Work now go to lunch later
5. Mr M Franklin Smith, Jr, lives in Pittsburgh, Pa
6. Dr Frank R Jackson, DDS, ordered these drills to be sent c o d
7. John R Boyd, Esq, was officially listed as "Sup't of Arsenals" and later as "Sec'y of War"
8. He gained $245 on his venture, but lost $15,324 later
9. Washington, DC, is north of Raleigh, NC
10. The merchandise went to Capt Johnson of Wallace Lines, Inc
11. We stayed at the YMCA in St Louis, Mo
12. Mrs Johnson asked Miss Smith to visit at noon
13. Norman Wells III received his BA from Yale and his PhD from Harvard
14. Won't you please come in, Mr. Smith
15. The US 4th Army Brigade is being transferred from Ft Dix, NJ, to St. Johns, BWI, aboard the USS Enterprise

Question Marks and Periods

A. Add question marks and periods wherever they are missing in the following sentences and in the letter below. Circle any letters that should be capitalized.

1. can you be there this evening
2. will you please allow me to pass
3. are you able to complete the exercises
4. why don't you use a carbon it will help
5. since our last order, have prices risen
6. i wonder why he was discharged
7. are you sure that all figures have been carefully examined and checked
8. he asked me where you are going tonight
9. can you name three generals in the u s army
10. why is he doing this, I wonder

Gentlemen:
    last may we ordered the new novel by george wilson, jr As yet we have not received it although it is already july 15 may we ask for an explanation
    is the book out of print or was our order simply misplaced If it is in stock, please ship it at once, cod If not, let us know when we can expect it
    rush
                                     very truly yours

Spelling hints: *Friend* ends in *end;* there is a *secret* in *secretary;* associate *governor* with *government* to help yourself spell and pronounce the *n* in *government.*

UNIT 19

periods, question marks, and exclamation points (3)

A. At the end of each of the following sentences, place a question mark, an exclamation point, or a period.

1. Did you send the letter
2. Please mail it at once
3. Won't you come in, please
4. Why wasn't it filed at once
5. A fine idea
6. The director asked many questions
7. Who is there
8. I am not sure who filed the letter
9. Will you be kind enough to visit us
10. Why not take a chance
11. Please leave immediately
12. What a charming child
13. Will he be coming
14. When will they meet
15. What will they discuss
16. Why
17. Can we doubt his sincerity
18. That is the $64,000 question
19. Amazing
20. What an amazing discovery
21. Did you see the shipment
22. Have they acknowledged our order
23. Wonderful
24. Won't you please consider our offer
25. This is wonderful news, isn't it
26. How can I help you
27. How beautiful
28. Will you please be seated
29. I don't understand. Do you
30. Do you think it was a good movie

Occurred and *occurrence* are very common words that many people have trouble spelling. If you cannot remember the rule about doubling the final consonant if a word (1) has the accent on the last syllable (oc*cur*) and (2) follows the consonant-vowel-consonant pattern (*pin*), and if the suffix begins with a vowel, memorize these two words to save yourself from looking them up in the dictionary every time you use them. Both have two -*c*'s and two -*r*'s.

If an abbreviation ends a sentence, only one period is used.

His dentist is Jose Gonzales, **D.D.S.**

There are abbreviations for most titles (*Mr., Dr.,* and so forth) and they are used in preference to writing out the words (*Mister,*

Doctor) when writing a title followed by a name. Periods follow the abbreviations. *Miss* is a complete word, not an abbreviation, and it is not followed by a period. Ordinal numbers (*1st, 100th*) are considered contractions rather than abbreviations, and they are not followed by periods. Contractions such as *Gen'l* that are written with apostrophes are not followed by periods.

        2nd Street   Gen'l   Sup't   Supt.   Gen.

B. Add the punctuation marks that are missing in the following sentences.

1. The shipment will be delivered by Friday
2. Bring it here
3. Order the goods immediately
4. Address the letter to Fulton Boyd, Esq
5. The shipment goes to Morris Van Lines, Inc
6. The plant is open for inspection all day (9 a m to 5:30 p m)
7. We received a c o d shipment from the Denver warehouse
8. Will you please let us hear from you in the very near future
9. Will you be at the banquet
10. The C P A examination is scheduled for early June
11. Are you certain that we can expect delivery of the merchandise by January 14 despite the newspaper's report that a strike may be called by the union at midnight on December 31
12. What a break I got a ten-dollar raise did you
13. The shipment is being sent c o d to Global, Inc
14. Will you please come in
15. It won't take long, will it

UNIT 19
periods, question marks, and exclamation points (4)

A. Add the correct punctuation to the following letter.

                                                  200 Woburn St
                                                  Greenville N C 27834
                                                  Jan 30 1973

Mr C D Howells
U S Publishing Co Inc
504 Fifth Ave
New York N Y 10036

Dear Mr Howells

    When I first received your letter, I thought "Good Heavens Does this fine publishing company actually plan to publish my trilogy and pay me only a six percent royalty " At that rate, I will be paid two dollars ($2 00) a day I have spent my entire life since the age of sixteen writing these three great novels and I am now eighty years old.
    After further thought, however, I have decided that the market for great trilogies is somewhat depressed lately, so would you please send the contract and the fifty dollar ($50) advance

                                                          Sincerely yours

                                                          Desdemona Glickman

Review

A. After each sentence, write the correct word in the parentheses.

1. His behavior was (as, like) that of a gentleman. _____
2. He acted (as, like) we would all wish to act in the circumstances. _____
3. The gunman said, "Either give me the money (and, or) I'll shoot." _____
4. "(Provided, Providing) you don't shoot, here is the money," the victim replied. _____
5. Please try (and, to) deliver the ordered goods by next Wednesday. _____
6. You will find that he not only harasses you (but, but also) persecutes you. _____
7. The piano was actually (as, so) loud as the radio. _____
8. Neither space (or, nor) time was sufficient for the demonstration. _____
9. You will receive not only six percent interest from our bank, (but, but also) a free back scratcher. _____
10. The president of the company said, "We try (and, to) make a profit." _____

B. Add commas where they are needed in the following sentences.

1. Although we made a profit this year we do not consider sales satisfactory.
2. The speaker went on and on even though most of the listeners were asleep.
3. We have no difficulty with the invoices but we would still like your help.
4. Although he could not understand it the treasurer read the profit and loss statement.
5. Highly paid executives and wealthy politicians are not immune from greed and corruption.

   Next time you are in a library browse through an unabridged dictionary to see how useful it is as a reference tool. In addition to the entries, you can find such tables as a table of measurements, a table of geological time, and the correct names for all the colors of the rainbow.

UNIT 19
periods, question marks, and exclamation points (5)

assignment

A. Add the necessary punctuation to the following letter.

                                                                               The Croft Co , Inc
                                                                               8700 Wilshire Blvd
                                                                               Beverly Hills, Calif 90211
                                                                              Nov 25, 1973

Mr Irving L De Marco
The Croft Co , Inc
2500 Greenville Rd
Homewood, Ill 60430

Dear Irving:

    Something really must be done about the deplorable situation caused by our seeming inability to deliver merchandise on time Is it caused by errors arising in our office Is the warehouse to blame for the delay These questions must be answered promptly and steps taken to correct the situation
    At the convention in Denver, Colo on Sept 5 of this year, salesmen were unable to make use of the booth we had paid for because they had no merchandise to display What a mess
    Will you please look into the reasons for shipping delays and let me know immediately what steps you are taking to correct them And I mean immediately

                                                                            Sincerely,

                                                                  Ms Theodora B Uckelheim

B. Rewrite the following letter, adding the correct punctuation.

                                      The Croft Co , Inc
                                      2500 Greenville Rd
                                      Homewood, Ill 60430
                                      Dec 30, 1973

Ms Theodora B Uckelheim
The Croft Co , Inc
8700 Wilshire Blvd
Beverly Hills, Calif 90211

Dear Ms Uckelheim:

    I gave your letter of Nov 25 prompt attention and can now report to you the causes for such delays as occurred at the Sept 5 convention in Denver, Colo
    Uncle Sam must bear part of the responsibility Do you realize how very slow postal service has been for the past few months The warehouse was responsible for the rest of the delay This office is in no way responsible for any of it Not at all
    I recommend that the warehouse be told to deliver all of our merchandise to a warehouse owned by my brother-in-law He will get the order out on time

                                          Sincerely,

                                          Irving L De Marco

UNIT 20
commas (1)

Introduction

Perhaps nothing is as sure a sign of a competent writer as his use of commas, and the way to use them correctly is to use them only when you have a definite reason. If you can't say why you need a comma in a particular place, you probably should leave it out. In this unit, we will discuss the most important uses of the comma.

When a series of three or more words is used in a sentence, there should be a comma after all but the last word.

>Our new offices are located in a **towering, ultra-modern, air-conditioned** skyscraper.
>
>**Wool, cotton, linen, or silk** will be used in the dress.

Use a comma (or a dash) after the last word in the series if it is followed by a complete sentence.

>**Courage, fortitude, and wisdom,** these are the strength of the nation.

Occasionally a series will be written with conjunctions between all the items, and commas should be omitted in this case.

>The meter has been carefully **and** precisely **and** painstakingly assembled.

A useful generalization that covers another use of commas is: Any word or words that could be omitted from the sentence without destroying its meaning should be set off with commas. This applies to the name of a person being addressed, words that explain other words, and participial phrases. Do not use commas if removing the expression would change the meaning of the sentence.

>Smith, **you are a good man.**
>**Mr. Jones,** President of Acme Steel, **is here.**
>**The architect,** seeing the finished building, **was elated.**

The same rule applies to relative clauses: If the clause can be removed without changing the meaning of the sentence, use commas. If not, don't.

>**Butter,** which is in great demand, **is selling well.**
>**Butter that is rancid doesn't taste good.**

This rule applies also to years in dates and states and countries in expressions of geographical locations as in the example sentences below. This is one of the most commonly broken rules of punctuation, however, and only a nitpicker will insist on the comma that comes *after* the state or country or after the year in a date. On the other hand, you may someday find yourself employed by a nitpicker!

> On January 15**, 1943,** he was accused of the crime.
> Fort Worth**, Texas,** was the scene of the crime.

Note that in the rule about using commas for any expression that could be removed from the sentence without destroying its meaning, we are speaking about commas that come in pairs. Unless the expression begins or ends the sentence, use two of them.

> **Having been dormant for years,** the company is finally reawakening.
> The company**, having been dormant for years,** is finally reawakening.

Commas Separating Items in a Series

A. Insert commas in the following sentences wherever necessary.

1. We will leave by car rail or plane on Friday.
2. The successful teacher is friendly alert interesting and self-confident.
3. Our store deals in radios TV sets refrigerators and similar products
4. We have correspondence from you dated August 3 August 18 September 6 and October 15.
5. You will not be able to resist our newest model when you see its long low streamlined appearance.
6. Newspapers magazines books and periodicals all will be on sale this week.
7. Our rates are $8.00 for a room without bath $10.50 for a room with bath and $18.00 for a suite of two rooms.
8. We deal in state bonds municipal bonds industrial bonds and railroad bonds.
9. We deal in state municipal industrial and railroad bonds.
10. Thirty days hath September April June and November.
11. We sell the finest kerosene benzene and alcohol lamps on the market.
12. The properties available are in Detroit St. Louis Cleveland and New York.
13. For lunch we offer roast beef salad and bread and butter.
14. Our courses include shorthand business English typewriting and bookkeeping.
15. She gave a stately prim correct appearance.
16. Would you be willing to spend a few dollars for a chance to break into a fast-growing profitable interesting respected profession?
17. Fame fortune and esteem—these were his lot in life.
18. Their firm deals in the finest silks cottons and woolens.
19. The box is neither lightweight nor presentable.
20. I can see now the lovely green lawn the broad gravel walk the giant shade trees and the perfect model of a colonial walk.

UNIT 20

commas (2)

Items in a Series; Names of Persons Addressed

A. Use commas to separate the items in the series in the following sentences.

1. The new skyscrapers have been luxuriously ornately and decoratively designed.
2. The efficient telephone operator answers pacifies informs and cajoles the caller.
3. I want you to learn to write to compose to correct and to dictate letters.
4. That a modern novelist is frank that he is imaginative and that he is perceptive are recognized facts.
5. Ask questions politely listen to details carefully and follow instructions intelligently.
6. Tact wisdom and diplomacy—these are necessities of an enlightened intelligent foreign policy.
7. Please try our new furniture polish.
8. To plan and design carefully to purchase and order wisely and to build and construct sturdily are necessary steps.
9. The firm of Webb Prince and Berman is well known.
10. He planned to invite workers farmers storekeepers salesmen etc.

B. Use commas to set off the names of persons directly addressed in the following sentences.

1. Thank you Mr. Shaw for the prompt attention given to our questionnaire.
2. We have directed Mr. James King of our credit department to discuss terms of payment with you.
3. They are being shown this week Mrs. Watson.
4. Mr. Adams we have learned that you will soon enjoy delivery of your new car.
5. I have looked further Mr. Grover into the Gray lumber situation.
6. Mr. Martin says that economic conditions will continue to be thoroughly sound.
7. Madam does the approach of warm weather suggest sending your furs to storage?
8. Is it the fault of this store that your account remains inactive Mrs. Wright?

9. Mr. White's inspection of our floor equipment was very helpful.
10. The January sales now being held throughout the store offer you exceptional values Mrs. Hays.

Explanatory Expressions

A. Insert commas wherever necessary in the following sentences.

1. Our representative from New Orleans Mr. A. J. Johnson is in town.
2. Asia the largest of the continents is becoming a major focus of international relations.
3. Our new location the corner of Sixth Avenue and 42nd Street is ideal for our type of business.
4. Our attorney Mr. G. A. Blake will call at your office tomorrow.
5. B. H. Brown golf champion of the South won the cup handily.
6. It is my pleasure to introduce H. Colin Phillips our friend and leader.
7. Would you enjoy living in a residential park a veritable winter wonderland of over 500 acres of high healthy beautifully wooded fertile land Mr. Smith?
8. We advise you to see either Mr. R. J. Jones Director of the Bureau or Mr. P. T. Smith his assistant.
9. The speakers were H. George Brittingham Professor of Business English and John Rogers Jr. Professor of American History.
10. The Mississippi America's longest river flows into the Gulf of Mexico.

A nonrestrictive clause is one that could be removed without changing the meaning of the sentence.

Nonrestrictive Clauses

A. Add commas to enclose the nonrestrictive clauses in the following sentences.

1. This morning we received a report from Mr. Johnson who is our representative in New York.
2. Wellington chalk which is the best chalk you can get is the most economical for school use.
3. Mr. Howard Clark who is president of the National Savings Association sent a copy of his latest address.
4. Our customers all of whom have been most kind to us will be pleased to hear of our latest plans.
5. The manufacture of this equipment which is the finest ever made is a painstakingly exact process.
6. These lessons which you should study every day will provide fine background for your future work.
7. Our office furniture all of which we bought last year is of ultra-modern design.
8. The new secretary who was trained at business school is the best we've ever had.
9. The luggage which was engraved with his initials was presented to Mr. Phillips.
10. The park which is noted for its old trees was established in 1889.

UNIT 20

commas (3)

A restrictive clause is one that *cannot* be removed without changing the meaning of the sentence. Restrictive clauses are not enclosed by commas.

Restrictive Clauses

A. Underline the restrictive clause in each of the following sentences.

1. The man who does a poor job does not last long in business.
2. The advertisement that catches the eye is the one that has a certain "plus."
3. Medicine is a profession that satisfies a man's desire to serve others.
4. Water that is stagnant is putrid.
5. Anyone who works hard can succeed.
6. Only those who are geniuses gain acclaim as musicians.
7. A rumor that we heard yesterday is disturbing.
8. The ledger that is in Room 217 is the one I want.
9. The officer who leads his men bravely gains their respect.
10. We observed a downward trend that is most unsatisfactory.

Explanatory Expressions

A. Each of the following sentences includes an explanatory expression. Some of the expressions should be set off by commas; others should not. Add commas to the sentences that require them.

1. Water that does not run rapidly becomes stagnant.
2. Your fall order which we received last week has been filled.
3. The man who runs the fastest wins the race.
4. John Doe who was tried for larceny was acquitted.
5. Deliver only those posters that you consider best as soon as you can.
6. The letter that was sent to him came back unopened.
7. This work which I feel sure you will enjoy is not very difficult.
8. The dress that I think you will like best has not yet arrived.
9. Our book is printed in type that is easy on the eye.
10. That woman who spoke to you at such great length yesterday is back.

The examples below show the use of commas when speaking of a person's son or daughter. Since, in the first example, if the word *Alan* were removed, the sentence would infer that he is an only son, the commas are necessary, providing, of course, that he

Page 169

is an only son. In the second sentence, the implication is that the person speaking has more than one son and he is using the son's name to identify which son he is speaking of.

My **son, Alan,** is attending college.
My **son Alan** is attending college.

B. If the explanatory expressions in the following sentences require commas, add them.

1. This business which you have merely sampled these past months can provide ample excitement for a lifetime.
2. A red-headed woman who does not have a fiery temper is a rarity.
3. Mr. Oglethorpe is a man who knows this business inside out.
4. The order which we have been awaiting for weeks was delayed again.
5. He is the man whom I would elect.
6. My teacher Frank C. Smith has been an inspiring influence.
7. I myself have much to study.
8. The poet Milton wrote about heaven.
9. Our business like any other new business will benefit from experience.
10. These data all of which are interesting do not change our business prediction.
11. Knowing that sales are the lifeblood of an organization we shall hire an alert salesman.
12. The new executives that lead our top organizations have youth and vitality.
13. They shipped the merchandise in May assuming you wanted it for June 15.
14. A sales letter that paints word pictures brings maximum results.
15. His brother Albert is brighter than his brothers John and Herman.

Certain conjunctions and phrases are customarily separated from the body of the sentence by commas. The following is a list of words and phrases of which this is true.

accordingly	meantime	still	for example
again	moreover	then	if any
also	namely	therefore	in fact
besides	naturally	too	in brief
consequently	next		in the first place
finally	nevertheless	as a rule	in other words
furthermore	notwithstanding	as you know	of course
hence	otherwise	at any rate	on the other hand
however	personally	by the way	on the contrary
indeed	respectively	I believe	that is

C. Add commas to the following sentences wherever necessary.

1. It is however unnecessary for you to reply at once.
2. Feel free of course to take as much time as you need.
3. Naturally we were shocked to hear of the delay.
4. It is nevertheless imperative that your representative contact us at once.
5. We feel on the other hand that your client is entitled to some minor sort of relief.

UNIT 20
commas (4)

A. Insert commas wherever necessary in the following sentences.

1. As we understand the situation, the failure was entirely the fault of your agent.
2. To be very frank, we were satisfied with neither the lamps, the shades, nor the fixtures.
3. It is, in our opinion, impossible to predict the outcome at this moment.
4. This class, however, is the best we have had.
5. No one, naturally, can be blamed for such an innocent mistake.
6. As a rule, commas should set off nonessential information.
7. I believe, for example, that a brusque answer does much harm and little good.
8. We feel, therefore, that politeness is an exemplary quality.
9. No, they did not report on time.
10. Well, all of us make mistakes.

When a question is added to a statement, a comma precedes it. When an opposing idea is added to a sentence and preceded with *not, seldom, few, never,* or similar words, a comma precedes such a word.

You sent the letter, **didn't you?**
Mr. Smith has gone to Chicago, **not** to St. Louis.

B. Add commas wherever necessary in the following sentences.

1. You received our catalogue, didn't you?
2. We will send you east, not west.
3. It's going to be a banner month, isn't it?
4. We shall judge a man by his accomplishments, not by his looks.
5. We offered you this line last year, didn't we?
6. You can do the job, can't you?
7. Look for facts, not opinions.
8. In treating employees, one should be kind and understanding, not rude and impatient.
9. This is easy, isn't it?
10. We hold most meetings in the morning, few in the afternoon.

Review

A. Add periods, question marks, and exclamation points wherever they are needed in the following sentences. Circle letters that should be capitalized.

1. do you know when the new models will be available
2. our new chairman is j p roberts
3. that's life
4. what a wonderful day
5. will you please bring the files into my office, miss jones
6. book sales are improving this is particularly true of paperbacks
7. you don't need to have a coffee break today, do you
8. at what time will the invoices be completed
9. the map indicates that denver, colo is east of los angeles, calif
10. alas our time is up
11. on wed , feb 11, the c a b (committee for american butter) will meet
12. can they deliver it by sept 17 I doubt it
13. cbs and nbc are among the best known tv networks
14. mrs flick is the president of flick products co , inc
15. inform the board members that next month's meeting will be in Chicago, Ill
16. dr dixon spends a great deal of time with his accountant
17. c p a 's have offices in the professional bldg
18. does air pollution affect the health of humans, horses, dogs, and birds
19. mr salvo will probably win the elections held on nov 10
20. are you sure that you sent me the bill

As business becomes increasingly international more and more secretaries will write letters to foreign addresses. Copy foreign addresses carefully, and be aware of how abbreviations and the placement of the elements of the addresses differ from those used in the United States.

namesectiondate

UNIT 20
commas (5)

assignment

A. Add the missing punctuation to the following letter.

>   The Even-Handed Life
>   Assurance Society
>   1275 Third Avenue
>   New York New York
>   May 7 1973

Dr Eugenia Williams
121 Prospect Street
Syracuse New York 13224

Dear Policyowner

    We'd like you to have our 1973 Annual Report. It is briefer and we believe more interesting than ever before.
    The Report notes that in 1972 we had outstanding sales results reached new highs in investment earnings and benefit payments to policyowners and our continuing efforts to develop more effective cost control mechanisms were also fruitful.
    Productivity of both agents and employees was up and we sought to make increasingly imaginative use of our resources including computer technology.
    If you would like a copy of the report please send us the enclosed card.

>   Sincerely yours

>   J Henry Eklund
>   Chairman of the Board

B. Rewrite the following letter, adding the correct punctuation and capitalizing any letters that should be capitalized.

The Even-Handed Life
Assurance Co , Inc
1275 3rd Ave
New York N Y
May 7 1973

Dr Eugenia Williams
121 Prospect St
Syracuse New York 13224

Dear Policyholder

    We are enclosing a copy of our 1973 Annual Report as you requested in it you will find that by year-end some 70% of our 3.5 million individual policies were incorporated into our computer-assisted policyowner service (CAPS) system which provides our 92 cashier's offices with direct access through a nationwide computer network to policyowner records CAPS is one of several efforts we are undertaking to strengthen our service to you.
    As you know Even-Handed functions for the benefit of our clients we try to do something with a working philosophy of effective service.

                      Sincerely yours

                      J Henry Eklund
                      president

If you have a handbook for secretaries, consult it often in order to become familiar with it. The more you use it, the more easily you will use it.

UNIT 21

colons, semicolons, and more about commas (1)

Introduction

In addition to its uses discussed in the preceding unit, commas are used to separate two complete thoughts connected by a coordinate conjunction such as *but, and, or, nor, yet*. In other words, in a compound sentence, place commas between all independent clauses.

> Our offer was made in good **faith, and** we trust you will give it full consideration.
> We are not prepared to act **now, nor** will we be prepared for many months.

Never place the comma after the conjunction in such a sentence.
Remember that a comma is not sufficient by itself to connect two separate complete thoughts. Replace it with a semicolon if you do not use a coordinate conjunction.

> Our offer was made in good **faith; we** trust you will give it full consideration.

Three or more complete thoughts may be joined with commas; however, the last comma should be followed by a coordinate conjunction.

> Our offer was made in good **faith,** it was made on **time, and** we trust you will give it full consideration.

Don't confuse a compound sentence with a sentence using a compound predicate. A compound sentence has two subjects, a compound predicate need not.

> **We** carefully set up our booth at the fair and arranged the displays attractively.
> **We** carefully set up our booth at the fair and **the public** was attracted by it.

Page 175

Whether or not a comma is used in a complex sentence depends on word order. If the independent clause comes first, the dependent clause does not usually require a comma before it. If the order is inverted, however, a comma is required.

> Since our offer was made in good **faith, we** trust you will give it full consideration.
> We trust you will give our offer full **consideration since** it was made in good faith.

A dependent clause must contain a predicate, and should not be confused with a prepositional phrase, which usually does not require a comma before or after it regardless of its position in the sentence.

> **At our last meeting** our offer was made in good faith.

In a few sentences, commas are used with prepositional phrases to prevent confusion.

> **Only three days before,** he came to New York.

The semicolon, as we saw above, may be used to separate two independent clauses.

> Prices **rose; wages** fell.

If a sentence is long or contains commas within independent clauses, a semicolon is necessary to separate the independent clauses even when they are connected by a coordinate conjunction.

> Naturally, having heard of the offer, he rushed to the employment office; but, despite his haste, he found that the job had already been filled.

For the same reason, a semicolon is used to separate items in a series when there are commas within the items.

> Our new Board of Directors is composed of **Rodney G. Jones, President; Augustus E. Smythe, Vice-President; and Ormand Cole, Jr., Secretary-Treasurer.**

The colon's use is easily learned since it is one of the least common punctuation marks. Use it after the salutation of a business letter, to introduce a long quotation, to introduce a list, and to separate hours from minutes when expressed in figures. Remember to use it after the salutation of a *business* letter even when the letter begins informally with a first name.

> Dear Mr. Jones: Dear Jack: 5:06 p.m.   6:30 a.m.
> Senator Jones replied as follows: "I know the importance of this investigation, but I would be ill-advised to become party to such a circus."
> The following invoices are unpaid: No. 3721, No. 3723, and No. 3746.

UNIT 21
colons, semicolons, and more about commas (2)

Except when using a colon, use a comma to set off a quotation from the rest of the sentence. When a comma ends the quotation, it goes inside the quotation marks.

>   He **said,** "I will not budge an inch."
>   "I will not budge an **inch,"** he said.
>   "Send the bill at **once,"** he threatened, **"or** there will be trouble."

A. Place commas where necessary in the following sentences.

1. He said "This is ridiculous."
2. "We shall not stop fighting" said he "nor shall we retreat an inch."
3. "Why" I asked "doesn't he admit he was wrong?"
4. "This is the worst job I have ever seen" was what he said.
5. I told him "Either you accept our offer or we shall deal elsewhere."
6. "Send the check to my office" he wrote.
7. "Who punched the clock at 5 P.M.?" he asked.
8. "Eureka!" he shouted at the top of his lungs "I have the solution."
9. General MacArthur swore that he would return.
10. He stated "I shall return!"
11. We have accomplished much since we started.
12. As soon as the clock struck five the employees stopped working.
13. Because there were extended coffee breaks management was irritated.
14. After hearing the good news he sold his stock.
15. He will not bargain unless you do so in good faith.

When a quotation is not a complete thought, omit the comma.

>   He said he **was "extremely** humiliated."

Page 177

B. Rewrite the following letter, using correct capitalization and punctuation.

My dear Miss Green:

Our hotel is a "once-in-a-lifetime" bargain.

The Drake Hotel is a comfortable and well-managed manor. Situated on a beautiful piece of land in the hills of Bell Harbor. From the heart of Baltimore it can be reached by train or automobile. In less than an hour. Although it is near the city. It is far enough removed for rest and quiet.

Majestic old trees and attractive walks add to the beauty of the grounds the extensive lawns reach to the shore of Chesapeake Bay fishing and boating are always in season.

If you can possibly arrange your vacation to fall in August you will find the Drake Hotel at its most beautiful flowers are in bloom and the shade trees are at their lushest. Of course some of our regular guests prefer the fall when the trees are ablaze with color. And the ground is covered with a thick carpet of fallen leaves.

We extend to you and your friends. A cordial invitation to visit us.

Sincerely

UNIT 21

colons, semicolons, and more about commas (3)

Other uses of commas include figures of more than 999, setting off titles that follow a person's name, and following abbreviations like *Inc.* at the end of a company name, as in the following examples.

    George Henry Smathers, **Jr., is** our President.
    Johnson and Johnson, **Inc., recently** published its latest profit figures.
    Elizabeth C. **Ramsey, LL.D., Ph.D., has** joined our faculty.

A. Add commas as necessary in the following sentences.

1. Last year our stockholders shared in profits of over $60000000.00.
2. On July 15 1964 the workers in our plants numbered 6475.
3. The contract dated August 4 1956 is still valid.
4. He has lived at 1220 Elm Avenue Springfield Illinois for eight years.
5. Despite poor January sales our overall net profit for the past year was over $250000.
6. We addressed the letter to Mrs. Robert Patterson 5202 South Spruce Avenue Madison Wisconsin.
7. Since our last visit in December 1963 we have reconsidered your $3000000 expansion plan.
8. We have reviewed your books for the month of July 1964 and we find a $3257.50 discrepancy with our figures.
9. On December 1 1964 we expect you to deliver 50000 tons of No. 10 steel to our warehouse at 1614 Bruce Avenue Pittsburgh Pennsylvania.
10. Please change my address in your listings from Polly Jones 616 Almond Street New Orleans Louisiana to Mrs. Robert Mayer 327 Elm Avenue Miami Beach Florida.
11. Ever since we have avoided telephoning.
12. Only three hours before we saw him alive.
13. It has been a long long process of waiting.
14. Whoever spoke spoke in vain.
15. Our arms budget exceeds $48000000000.
16. September 3 1912 was the date of the founding of the company.
17. July 4 1776 was a red-letter day for the U.S.

18. The affair last Wednesday August 17 was a huge success.
19. The issue for July 1964 is a particularly interesting one.
20. John James III has lived at 373 Ocean Avenue San Francisco California for five years.

B. Insert colons and commas wherever necessary in the following sentences.

1. We have recorded your order as follows one wooden cabinet one chair three metal files one desk.
2. He is quoted as saying "My only regret is that I have but one life to give for my country."
3. At precisely 456 p.m. our plane departs.
4. The following is stock on hand 3000 #10 envelopes, 2500 #13, and 1500 #17.
5. This is what he said "No amount of money could ever repay you for the fine unselfish job you did on behalf of your nation."
6. The letter began "Dear Sir I wish to thank you for your help."
7. The President stated "My fellow Americans I speak to you today on a matter of grave importance."
8. The problems we must face are these avoiding nuclear war upholding liberty developing free societies.
9. We listed three stock prices $5.52 $5.59 $6.01.
10. The following furniture was ordered three tables four chairs and four sofas.

C. Insert semicolons and commas wherever necessary in the following sentences.

1. We have not received your exam as yet consequently we have delayed sending your next lesson.
2. This is a fine surprise we were just thinking of you.
3. We have done our best the rest is up to you.
4. There are two reasons for our decision namely your determination and your doggedness.
5. To be perfectly frank I am sorry to see him go but I know that try as you might you had no alternative but to fire him.
6. The market went up for some stocks others, however, declined in value.
7. All of us were concerned about the employment picture for the year as presented by the government but following your advice we felt it our duty to remain calm.
8. Our Society includes James Brown the eminent painter Jack Jules the famous caricaturist and Cynthia Prince the well-known columnist.
9. He had one principle namely to do unto others before they did unto him.
10. The manager spoke to the staff about staying late however it was to no avail.

UNIT 21

colons, semicolons, and more about commas (4)

Review

A. Rewrite the following letter with the correct punctuation marks. The letter is continued on the next page. (Use an extra sheet of paper if necessary.)

Gentlemen:

Your letter and the booklet "Live Records" reach us at a time when our bookkeeping system is a matter of great concern This booklet therefore has received our careful attention

Since our office force was reduced last year the marked development of business during the past year has increased the urgency of our bookkeeping problem Though we have been considering the use of bookkeeping machines for a long time we are not yet convinced however that such a large outlay of money would result in a satisfactory return Nevertheless something must be done to relieve the pressure which is becoming great of our work

Will you have your representative Mr. Roberts call on Monday May 10 at ten o'clock to discuss arrangements

Think before you use a sentence with a negative to prevent a double negative (*I don't want any* not *I don't want none*).

This is a continuation of the letter begun on page 181. Rewrite it using the correct punctuation marks.

It is our intention to have Mr. Roberts examine our ordering billing and shipping procedures. Above all we want him to meet our bookkeepers and clerks and after he forms an impression of them we would like him to submit a written report of his recommendations with respect to personnel This would seem to be a reasonable approach wouldn't it

Are you aware of the many many new products that are being offered by our firm to customers throughout North America Central America and South America Since January 1963 we have been involved in a $3000000 expansion of our product line that has succeeded despite great odds Today we stand first in volume of sales in this field and we intend to maintain this position

Our problem is to handle the bookkeeping load and that I believe is exactly what your firm can help us achieve We look forward therefore to Mr. Roberts' visit

                                                        Sincerely

To improve pronunciation and grammar, listen to a model speaker every day and practice repeating some of his sentences aloud.

UNIT 21
colons, semicolons, and more about commas (5)

A. Rewrite the following letter adding the necessary punctuation marks.

Standard Products Co Inc
267 N Wells St
Chicago Ill 60606
June 16 1973

Miss A B Nielson
365 E Blossom Rd
Carport N H 03102

Dear Miss Nielson

    Have you considered a new color television for your home If you have don't decide on the brand until you have seen the Standard What a beautiful picture it gives
    Your local dealer will be glad to give you a free demonstration and you will be delighted with what you see Since we have one million satisfied customers we know that we can satisfy you
    So don't delay See the Standard television in color today

                Sincerely

                J D Kline
                President

B. Rewrite the following letter adding the necessary punctuation.

365 E Blossom Rd
Carport N H 03102
June 20 1973

Standard Products Co Inc
267 N Wells St
Chicago Ill 60606

Dear Mr Kline

    I received your sales letter about your new color TV and you are absolutely right Your merchandise is excellent What a fine product
    Do you have a model less expensive than the $1 000.99 model I saw While I was pleased with the demonstration that is a little more money than I planned to pay
    Will you please send your answer soon since I am anxious to buy my new set

Very truly yours

(Miss) A B Nielson

One reason that almost everyone has to use a dictionary to spell every word correctly is to be found in the fact that although our language has forty sounds, it has only twenty-six letters. Many of the letters must do double duty. Our vowel letters (*a, e, i, o, u,* and sometimes *w* and *y*) must stand for sixteen sounds, and that is why vowel letters are particularly troublesome.

Page 184   colons, semicolons, and more about commas (5)

UNIT 22
quotation marks, apostrophes, and hyphens (1)

Introduction

Use quotation marks to enclose a direct quotation. A direct quotation repeats the exact words of what was originally said or written. An indirect quotation is not enclosed in quotation marks. The sentence on the left below contains a direct quotation. The one on the right, an indirect quotation.

> He said, "I am going."   He said that he was going.

Note that the period comes inside the quotation marks in the first sentence above. A comma rather than a period is used if a complete sentence that is quoted does not end the sentence.

> "I am going," he said.

When a complete quoted sentence is broken into more than one part, both parts are enclosed in quotation marks. Do *not* begin the second part of the quoted sentence with a capital.

> "Send us the bill," he writes, **"and** we will mail you a check by return mail."

When recording the direct conversation of two or more people, place the quotations in separate quotation marks and in separate paragraphs.

Quotation marks are also used around the title of an article or chapter in a magazine, newspaper, or book. The name of the magazine, newspaper, or book is usually underlined or written in all capital letters.

> NEWSWEEK had an article last month titled "The News in the Nation's Capital."

Quotation marks are also used around unusual words, coined phrases, or colloquial expressions.

> Our sales staff must be "on-the-ball."

It is incorrect to use quotation marks to emphasize a word. Use underlining instead.

Page 185

Apostrophes are used to form contractions and to form the possessive case of a noun. When apostrophes are used in contractions, the apostrophe should be placed where letters were left out. Think of the two words that make the contraction in order to decide which letters have been left out.

When forming the possessive of a noun that does not end in -s, add apostrophe and -s, whether the word is singular or plural.

> The **child's** toys are upstairs.
> The **children's** department is on the first floor.

Remember that the possessive form of a pronoun (*hers, his, theirs*) never takes an apostrophe.

If the noun ends in -s, whether it is singular or plural, add an apostrophe.

> Mr. **Jones'** house is at two **streets'** intersection.

Use the hyphen to divide a word that cannot be completed at the end of a line. The modern business practice is to avoid dividing words when possible; that is, if the margin at the right can be kept reasonably straight without dividing any words, do not divide them. A line of type five spaces shorter or three spaces longer than the margin is acceptable.

The only way to be sure you are hyphenating correctly is to consult your dictionary. Look at the boldface entry word to find the correct division, not at the pronunciation guide that follows the entry—the entry and the pronunciation guide may not be the same. A few general rules for dividing words: Divide after a prefix (*con-clude, un-necessary, inter-rupt*) and before a suffix (*forc-ible, hope-less, wish-ing*). Divide between double letters unless part of the word is a complete word (*rub-ber,* but *small-est*). Divide between the words that make up a compound word (*never-theless, how-ever*).

This unit deals also with those compound words that are always hyphenated, whether or not they come at the end of a line (*attorney-at-law, self-criticism*).

Use a colon to introduce a direct quotation of one long sentence or of two or more sentences regardless of length. Use a comma to introduce a direct quotation of a short sentence or of part of a sentence.

> The President declared**:** "In a time of peril such as this we must jealously guard our liberties and defend our national integrity against all encroachments."
> The President said**,** "I am confident of victory."

UNIT 22

quotation marks, apostrophes, and hyphens (2)

If a quotation consists of more than one paragraph, quotation marks are repeated at the beginning of each paragraph. They are *not* repeated at the end of each paragraph, but only at the end of the last paragraph of the quotation.

> The letter read: "We received your recent order and wish to thank you for it. You should be receiving your shipment shortly.
> "You may also be interested in a new line of fabrics. We are enclosing samples of these fabrics."

Single quotation marks are used to enclose a quotation within a quotation.

> He said, "I believe the old saying, 'Haste makes waste.'"

Here are the rules for placing other punctuation marks inside or outside of quotation marks:

A final comma or period always goes *inside* the quotation marks.

A final colon or semicolon always goes *outside* the quotation marks.

Question marks, exclamation points, and dashes are placed *inside* the quotation marks if they refer to the quotation itself; they are placed *outside* the quotation marks if they refer to the entire sentence.

A. Punctuate the following sentences correctly, referring to the rules above.

1. He said Let the chips fall.
2. Give me the statistics Jones retorted and I'll have the answer in a minute.
3. Here is a list of causes cited in The Rising Cost of Living higher wages, increased tariffs, lower rates of productivity.
4. The encircled troops were told Surrender or die they chose to fight on.

Page 187

5. Will you join me he asked.
6. Wow was all he could say.
7. Our flight position is were the pilot's last recorded words.
8. Did you read our article The Higher Light
9. Congratulations on your latest article How to Invest
10. To be or not to be . . . Shakespeare.
11. Do you remember the page on which the word occurred in Selling for Profit
12. Have you received the letter he asked
13. This is beautiful he exclaimed.
14. Did you enjoy the article Raising Minks for Fun and Profit
15. He asked How many books do you have on this subject

The Apostrophe

Use the apostrophe to form the plural of letters and numbers.

> *Mississippi* has four *i*'s, four *s*'s, and two *p*'s.
> We ordered a new shipment of No. 105's.

A. Rewrite the following letter adding the necessary punctuation marks. The letter continues on the next page.

Dear Miss Roberts:

    We cant understand the failure of your firms representative to visit any of our shops during his two-week visit to our city. Its apparent to us that your sales staff misunderstands our companys position in this city. Were not a small chain of widely separated stores. Ours is a large organization with no two stores more than ten blocks apart and one of them more than a few minutes walk from the center of town.
    Our figures for the past half years sales reflect this concentration in our citys prime market area. These sales figures show that ours is a very profitable operation. Ones personal tastes shouldnt influence his decisions in business matters. Hard facts and figures should be the businessmans only criteria.

UNIT 22

quotation marks, apostrophes, and hyphens (3)

A. The following is a continuation of the letter begun on page 188.
Rewrite it, adding the necessary punctuation marks.

    Well be very much pleased to open our books and records to your firm at your representatives convenience. Wouldnt you be foolish to let this opportunity go by unnoticed? Its not too late to change your mind.
    Each of our shops has its own individual management and its own individual personality. All of them are famous for their consistently fine goods—the best in mens womens and childrens clothing.
    Were justly proud of the reputation weve established among our towns most respected people. Wont you please accept this invitation to send one of your representatives to inspect our stores and our books. Were looking forward to your reply within a few days time.

                                              Sincerely,

Spelling hint: The verse about *i* and *e* is useful enough to be worth memorizing:
    I before *e* except after *c*
    And when sounding like *ay*
    As in *neighbor* and *weigh*.

Hyphens

The following words may not be divided at the end of a line:
    1. words of one syllable (*talked, through*);
    2. two-syllable words with fewer than six letters (*ago, elate*); two-syllable words with a syllable that has only one letter (*arouse*);
    3. proper nouns (Mr. Fedesco), contractions, or abbreviations;
    4. numerals;
    5. the last word in a paragraph or on a page.
At least three letters should be carried over when you divide (*con-sumer*, not *consum-er*). Divide hyphenated compound words only at a point where a hyphen naturally occurs (*sister-in-law*).

A. Write each word as it should be divided at the end of a line. If the word cannot be divided, do not write anything. Consult your dictionary if necessary.

EXAMPLE: problem   prob-lem

1. narrate _____
2. hopeful _____
3. natural _____
4. inert _____
5. legible _____
6. consist _____
7. although _____
8. operate _____
9. forward _____
10. biggest _____
11. convince _____
12. believe _____
13. cupful _____
14. season _____
15. rental _____
16. amount _____
17. message _____
18. question _____
19. innate _____
20. remove _____
21. reveal _____
22. tomato _____
23. insist _____
24. invoice _____
25. result _____
26. ahead _____
27. forget _____
28. desirable _____
29. plastic _____
30. placate _____

UNIT 22

quotation marks, apostrophes, and hyphens (4)

Hyphenated Words

Compound words that begin with *self* always take a hyphen after *self* (*self-conscious*). Compound words made up of a prefix plus a capitalized noun (*ex-President*) are always hyphenated. When expressions like *up to date* come before the noun they modify, they are usually hyphenated: (*We have an up-to-date system*). When they do not come before the word they modify, they are usually not hyphenated: (*Our system is up to date*). However, dictionaries differ greatly on hyphenating. For the sake of consistency, your own dictionary is your best guide on hyphenating.

A. Some of the following words are written as two words, with a space between them. Some have a hyphen between the word parts. Some are written as one word, with no space between them. Use your dictionary to determine the correct spelling, then rewrite each word or each two words.

EXAMPLES: self evident   <u>self-evident</u>   letter head   <u>letterhead</u>

1. self control _____
2. father in law _____
3. can not _____
4. real estate _____
5. first class _____
6. inter American _____
7. mountain side _____
8. news caster _____
9. cold blooded _____

10. forty six _____
11. inter national _____
12. master plan _____
13. per cent _____
14. over do _____
15. how ever _____
16. vice chairman _____
17. all right _____
18. not withstanding _____

Page 191

19. broad minded _____ 25. ice cream _____
20. hit and run _____ 26. lake side _____
21. labor saving _____ 27. news stand _____
22. never the less _____ 28. over due _____
23. notary public _____ 29. there after _____
24. fire proof _____ 30. work shop _____

Review

A. Commas, periods, and question marks have been left out of the following paragraph. Insert them wherever necessary.

It is our intention to have Mr Roberts examine our ordering billing and shipping procedures Above all we want him to meet our bookkeepers and clerks and after he forms an impression of them we would like him to submit a written report of his recommendation with respect to personnel This would seem to be a reasonable approach wouldn't it

B. Colons, semicolons, commas, and periods have been left out of the following sentences. Insert the necessary punctuation marks and circle the letters that should be capitalized.

1. We offer a choice of three models the stately Classical the functional Colonial or the streamlined Modern.
2. Once again we are extending the time however in the future there will be no further extension
3. Standing up in the Assembly Patrick Henry shouted "Give me liberty or give me death"
4. Mrs. Housewife just mail the enclosed card postage is prepaid
5. The traits that I most admire in a man are these honesty wisdom and perseverance
6. During the past few months which have been especially hectic I inspected the following divisions the Tennessee factory the Missouri offices and the Louisiana warehouse
7. Therefore we are pleased to be able to extend this invitation but bear in mind that much as we would prefer that it be otherwise this must be our last offer
8. You Mr Smith have already received our final offer henceforth we shall not bother you again
9. To err is human to forgive divine.
10. Since our last report we have restudied the figures you submitted but despite our attempts to reconcile them the surplus figures do not coincide.

UNIT 22

quotation marks, apostrophes, and hyphens (5)

assignment

A. Quotation marks and other punctuation marks have been left out of the following sentences. Insert all necessary punctuation marks and circle the letters that should be capitalized.

1. he told his secretary Marie give your full attention to this purchase order.
2. do you manufacture these they asked
3. he spoke with authority saying you may be certain that our firm adheres only to the highest standards of business ethics
4. your article southeast asia has created a stir.
5. did you receive any compensation for writing the coming battle of congress
6. he asked the question how can we justify our own failure to help them
7. of all the men I know he said none compares with mr jones
8. try our new air conditioner the ad stated it will bring comfort to your home or office
9. the enclosed booklet make your own weather will show you how to maintain your volume of business during summer months
10. how are sales for your book make your own weather
11. in your letter you write that the price of shipment will soon go up
12. Shakespeare wrote the evil that men do lives after them the good is oft interred with their bones
13. Nathan Hale shouted my only regret is that I have but one life to give for my country
14. don't give up the ship the commander bellowed.
15. let us know by return mail he wrote whether you will accept the offer.

Most of the people you hear on radio and television have trained themselves to speak clearly and to use standard English. That is why they make excellent models

Page 193

for anyone who wants to improve his pronunciation or to learn standard English. Each night, listen to a news announcer and find one word you usually mispronounce, then practice saying it properly several times. Your speech should improve steadily.

B. After each sentence, write the correct word in parentheses.

1. (It's, Its) a wonderful opportunity for you. _____
2. Can this be (yours, your's)? _____
3. (Your, You're) offer is most interesting. _____
4. The (women's, womens') coats are in here. _____
5. (There, They're) are three reasons for this decision. _____
6. Give them (their, they're) due. _____
7. (They're, Their) fed up with this type of bickering. _____
8. Send us a gross of (No. 10s, No. 10's) and a hundred (No. 17s, No. 17's). _____
9. A (mans, man's) success is measured in terms other than money. _____
10. The company sent (its, it's) form letter. _____
11. He is working in the (children's, childrens) department. _____
12. He runs a (men's, mens) shoe store. _____
13. The company is proud of (it's, its) reputation. _____
14. Remember to dot your (*i*'s, *i*s) and cross your (*t*'s, *t*s). _____
15. (Who's, Whose) paper is this? _____

UNIT 23

parentheses, dashes, and ellipses (1)

Introduction

Parentheses are used to enclose expressions that are incidental, explanatory, or supplementary to the main thought of a sentence.

> You have already learned **(see Unit 6)** about verb tenses.

When a sentence ends with an expression in parentheses, place the period after the parenthesis. When a sentence in parentheses is an independent thought, it starts with a capital letter and ends with the period inside the parenthesis.

> We agree to accept payment of eight hundred dollars **($800.00).**
>
> The invoices will be completed on Thursday. **(Mary will see to this.)** They will be mailed on Friday.

The use of the dash is somewhat similar to that of parentheses. It indicates a major break in the continuity of thought, and, like parenthetical expressions, it can usually be removed and leave a complete sentence.

> The large house—**and it was extremely large**—stood on the corner.

The dash is also used instead of a comma to emphasize an explanatory phrase. If not overused, it is an effective way of catching the reader's eye.

> America—**that bastion of democracy**—has an obligation to the world.

Except in a sentence like *We want to tell you about our product—the Schenley car,* in which the expression after the first dash ends the sentence, it is important to remember that dashes, like parentheses, come in pairs. Not *Our product—the Schenley car, is gaining in popularity,* but

> Our product—**the Schenley car**—is gaining in popularity.

A dash may punctuate your sentence more clearly if an explanatory aside must include commas.

> Our products—**automobiles, trucks, and trailers**—mean quality.

In this case, it is particularly important to use the second dash.

The other important use of a dash is before the name of an author when that name is placed after a quotation.

> Unbroken happiness is a bore; it should have ups and downs.—**Moliere**

The preferred way to indicate a dash on a typewriter (since most typewriters do not have this character) is to strike the hyphen twice, with no space between it and the words before and after it.

> The officers--the President, the Vice-President, and others--have approved of the plans.

Another way (use it if it is the style approved by your company) is a single hyphen with a space before and after.

> The officers - the President, the Vice-President, and others - have approved of the plans.

Ellipses are three dots used in a direct quotation to indicate that part of the quotation has been left out. If the omitted material is at the end of a sentence, a fourth dot representing the period is added.

> If a man has freedom enough to live healthy . . . he has enough.—Goethe
>
> Kant said: "Freedom is that faculty which enlarges the other faculties . . . ."

Parentheses and Brackets

Brackets are similar to parentheses, but are used in a special situation. They are used in direct quotations to indicate matter that has been inserted by the editor and does not appear in the original quotation. They frequently serve to clarify the original material.

> The minister quoted the proverb: "The exception proves [tests] the rule."

In the above sentence, *tests* gives the modern word for which *prove* was once used.

If a sentence, with a parenthetical expression deleted, would have a comma, place the comma after the second parenthesis.

> After leaving (we left in a **hurry**), we caught the plane.

A. In each sentence, insert parentheses or brackets around the word or words that require them.

1. There is no possibility so I am told that this deal will be consummated.
2. I have told the Director that you will have the goods delivered by Tuesday. John please be sure that you get the goods there on time. He will accept shipment then.
3. His latest article "Lost Opportunities" is certain to receive an award.
4. This offer and it is our final offer is too good to be refused.
5. Wherefore why art thou Romeo?

UNIT 23

parentheses, dashes, and ellipses (2)

Parentheses in an Itemized List

In a sentence containing an itemized list, parentheses are used to enclose letters or numbers to indicate that the item after it is part of a running list. If the list is long, it is more usual to allow each item its own line, however. In that case, either a single parenthesis or a period is used after the letter or number.

Practice serves to **(a)** improve your coordination, **(b)** increase your speed, and **(c)** develop your strength.

Practice serves to
a) improve your coordination
b) increase your speed
c) develop your strength.

Practice serves to
a. improve your coordination
b. increase your speed
c. develop your strength.

A. Referring to the above, show two other ways of writing the following information.

In order to obtain a driver's license, you must
a. show your birth certificate
b. complete a written examination
c. pass a road test
d. pass a vision test

_____

_____

_____

_____

Parentheses, Dashes, and Commas

A. Each of the following sentences contains an expression that could be left out without changing the meaning of the sentence. Decide whether parentheses, dashes, or commas should enclose each expression, and add the punctuation.

EXAMPLE: The Amazon Basin, which is one of the last wild areas of the world, is already being destroyed by technology.

1. The truth at least I think it's the truth is that Robinson has violated our trust.
2. We are proud of that symbol of free enterprise the New York World's Fair.
3. In one of his most famous plays Hamlet Shakespeare's hero said, "To be or not to be—that is the question."
4. Our advertising agency Smith, Smith, Smith, and Smith has outlined a rather banal campaign.
5. The salesmen Mr. Corboy, Ms. Dabkowski, and Mr. Mendham will meet at 9 A.M.
6. The electric appliances these include stoves, refrigerators, toasters, and television sets are among the most reasonably priced in the city.
7. Dr. Elizabeth Van I assume you know of her was given a degree at the time when I graduated.
8. The children who come from many ethnic backgrounds all enjoy their trip to the circus.
9. The helicopter one of the latest can be seen at the airport.
10. Our company it is one of the oldest in the country does a million dollar business annually.

Ellipses

A. Rewrite each of the following sentences, substituting ellipses for the underlined phrases.

EXAMPLE: A quiet <u>but profound and perhaps permanent</u> change is taking place in political life <u>in this country</u>.
_____A quiet . . . change is taking place in political life . . . ._____

1. A sharp reduction in the backlog of criminal cases <u>and a consequent decline in the number of defendants</u> resulted in a large saving of money.

2. The mayor announced the appointment of Dr. Smith, <u>a professor of history at the university</u>, to head the department of sanitation.

3. <u>Encouraged by the initiative in the industry,</u> the President's National Commission pressed for many new innovations.

4. Last month the nation's airlines reached tentative agreement with unions <u>on an 8-month contract before a moratorium on strikes expired.</u>

5. <u>Highly regarded</u> Man-O'War finished third <u>at the nationally famous racetrack</u> at Aqueduct yesterday <u>as Secretariat won the race.</u>

If a word begins with a silent letter, you may have difficulty looking it up in the dictionary. Learn the combinations of letters that stand for sounds. The sound that begins *fat,* for example, is spelled *ph* in words of Greek origin (*photo*). The sound that begins *sat* is spelled *ps* in words of Greek origin (*psyche*).

UNIT 23

parentheses, dashes, and ellipses (3)

A. Add the necessary parentheses, dashes, and hyphens in the following sentences. Use your dictionary if necessary to determine which words to hyphenate.

1. It is self evident at least it should be so to a reasonable man that our economic outlook is brightening.
2. Please look at our advertisement you can find one in this month's issue of the New Era to see what we mean by vibrant layout.
3. You should be able to collect the facts and we mean all the facts with little trouble if you are willing to apply yourself.
4. And the Licensee hereby agrees to pay Licensor on the first day of each month commencing on January the first Nineteen hundred and sixty five the sum of one hundred dollars $100.00.
5. As you have already learned see Unit 5 a pronoun should agree in person and number with its antecedent.
6. We are interested I might say extremely interested in the report of those men who attended your factory demonstration.
7. As a result of our long experience never forget we have been in business for over a hundred years we feel it our duty to urge you to reconsider your decision.
8. Our representative Mr. Fred Perry didn't you meet him at our last convention will be glad to assist you in any way possible.
9. This chance and it's your very last chance is a fine opportunity.
10. Practice to a listen carefully b speak clearly c make your point.
11. Ex-Governor Brown you must have heard of him gave the opening speech.
12. Ms. Miller an excellent typist introduced the governor.
13. Rock music it is quite different from classical music was played at the concert.
14. Our product a product we are sure you will want to try is available next week.
15. Our star salesman Mr. Luigi we are very proud of him received an award.

Review

A. Rewrite the following paragraphs with the correct punctuation.

Memorandum to J. P. Roberts

We received a letter from Modern Offices, Inc., that reads as follows:

Gentlemen: We have your letter of June 15, in which you enclosed the specifications for the safe equipment to be installed in the new offices of the Martin Manufacturing Company.

We shall be glad to send you pictures and details of Western safes that meet these requirements.

It would be more convincing, however, to have you and your customer visit us in Cleveland. May we, therefore, extend an invitation to you and your customer to come to Cleveland at our expense?

Please let us know when it will be most convenient for you, and we shall make the necessary hotel reservations.

Cordially yours,

In view of the invitation extended to us in this letter, I think we should very seriously consider sending a representative to inspect the Western safes in Cleveland.

Page 200 — parentheses, dashes, and ellipses (3)

UNIT 23
parentheses, dashes, and ellipses (4)

assignment

A. The article on this page and on page 202 omits punctuation marks that you have studied. Rewrite it with the correct punctuation. (Use a blank sheet of paper if more space is needed.)

HOW BANKS OPERATE

The ordinary idea of a bank is of an institution where one deposits money for safekeeping and withdraws it as it is needed There are many people who think of a bank in no other terms who give no thought to the manner in which a bank profits by these operations

The two fundamental concerns of a bank are borrowing and lending money When you deposit money in a bank whether it is in a checking or a savings account you are lending it money The bank in turn lends this money or a part of it to others at a rate of interest that is higher than that which you receive The difference is the profit made by the bank Such an institution must keep a surplus on hand with which to accommodate your withdrawals or the checks that you issue

> **The sound that begins *kill* is sometimes spelled *ch* (*chemistry*), and *c* is a more common spelling for this sound than is *k*. If the sound after initial sound /k/ is short *e* or short *i* (*kick*, *kettle*), however, look under *k* in the dictionary.**

This is a continuation of the article on page 201. Rewrite it with the necessary punctuation marks.

    As a general rule a checking account balance draws no interest The depositor receives service for the use of his money A savings account however draws a small rate of interest and the bank profits by lending your money at a higher rate than it pays
    Another commonly used service of a bank is provision of storage facilities for money securities important papers jewels and other valuables These are guarded in what is known as a safe deposit vault a place that is rented for a certain sum per year for this purpose
    Banks sell service They hire borrow money and they rent lend money When one hires money he has to pay the rent which is interest He also has to provide collateral or security which may be sold in case the money is not repaid
    In addition the banks offer many other services to their clients or customers They collect drafts checks and coupons from bonds they pay checks issued by depositors they extend credit and they act as trustees administrators executors and guardians They advise clients with regard to the investment of money in securities land or business of any kind They are usually able to advise and assist in all kinds of financial transactions

UNIT 24

capitalization (1)

Introduction

For the sake of completeness, you are reminded here of something you have been observing for as long as you remember: Sentences, including questions, begin with a capital letter, and the proper names of persons and places (*John Doe, Chicago, Illinois*) also begin with capital letters.

You probably have also mastered most of the rules that follow. Read them and study those that are not yet second nature to you.

Capitalize the first word of a direct quotation if it is a complete sentence. If the direct quotation is not a complete sentence, do not capitalize it.

> He said, **"This** job must be improved upon."
> He said that the job **"must** be improved upon."

Traditionally the first word in a line of poetry is capitalized, but this rule does not necessarily apply to modern poetry. The only way to be sure of capitalization in this case is to see the source from which the poem was taken.

Capitalize the word *dear* in a salutation when it comes at the beginning of the salutation, not otherwise.

> **Dear** Sir: **Dear** Mr. Jones: My dear Mr. Jones:

Capitalize *only* the first word in the complimentary close of a letter.

> **Sincerely** yours,   **Yours** sincerely,   **Very** truly yours,

This unit will deal with some of the finer points of capitalizing in the following pages. Remember, however, that when you are in doubt, your dictionary can be your guide. If a word should be capitalized, most dictionaries capitalize the bold-face entry, so all you need to do is find the entry in the dictionary. (An exception to this practice is the unabridged dictionary *Webster's Third New International Dictionary of the English Language, Unabridged.* This dictionary presents all entries in lower case letters. Words that you will want to capitalize will be followed by the abbreviation *usu cap,* meaning *usually capitalized.*)

Capitalizing Titles and Organizations

Although your dictionary can usually tell you which words to capitalize, there are some words that are lower or upper case depending on how they are used. When titles refer to a specific person, they are capitalized. When they refer to an office rather than a person, they are not capitalized.

> The **President** is not at the White House.
> He serves as **President** Nixon's Press Secretary.
> The United States has had thirty-seven **presidents.**
> School **Superintendent** Jones addressed the other **superintendents.**

When *company, corporation, committee,* or any other word for an organization is used as the name for an organization, it is capitalized. If it is not part of a specific organization's name, it is not capitalized.

> The Acme **Company** has had an increase in earnings.
> We deal with many **companies** like Acme.
> A committee has been formed to prevent drug addiction.
> He belongs to the **Anti-Drug Addiction Committee.**

When names of organizations are abbreviated, they retain the capitalized first letter.

When a geographic term is used as part of the name of a specific mountain, river, valley, or other geographic place, capitalize it when it comes after the name. If it comes before the name, do not capitalize it except in the case of the word *mount*.

> Hudson River   The river Jordan
> Pacific Ocean   The valley of the river Nile
> Mount Everest
> Mount Whitney

A. Using the above information and your dictionary, correct the capitalizations in the following sentences.

1. The Medlock tool co. appreciates the Information it received from you on october 17.
2. Our Local board of education requests bids on the new School.
3. The Boardman vocational institute has a new superintendent, samuel Jones.
4. Allen and white, inc., received your Order for the Fall line early in September.
5. Mr. Robert c. Phillips, chairman of the Firm of Phillips and sons, intends to open up the west as its newest market.
6. the Carlsbad hotel is located South of Main street.
7. The Advertising Agency of Bemis, Baumer, and Beard offers exceptional coverage throughout the northwest.
8. We have inquired of our Attorney, mr. john l. dowings, to ascertain our Rights against the Omega insurance co.
9. The assistant director of The Lakeland hotel is john doe, jr.
10. The president left the white house by Limousine at Noon and rushed to the airport.
11. The Bookkeeper passed his c.p.a. Examination.
12. Our vice-president went south for the Winter.
13. The u.s.s. president Pierce is in its Berth in liverpool, england, ready for a difficult crossing of the atlantic ocean.
14. The american society for the prevention of cruelty to animals is known as the a.s.p.c.a.

UNIT 24

capitalization (2)

When a direction (*north, south, east, west*) is named, do not capitalize it. When these and similar words refer to a section of the United States (*North, Southeast*), capitalize them. Names derived from a section of the United States are also capitalized, as are adjectives (*Eastern*) derived from names of large areas of the earth (*The Far East*).

> After living all his life in the **Northeast,** he decided to go **southwest.**
> He is a **Southerner,** but he has lived in **Western Europe** for years.

When *northern, western,* and so forth do not refer to a large area of the earth, they are not capitalized.

> After living in **Western Europe,** he moved to **northwestern California.**

Words similar to *hotel, street, tunnel,* and *revolution* are capitalized when they are part of a name, but not otherwise.

> While living in the **New Yorker Hotel,** he was writing on the **French Revolution.**

Apply this logic to schools, governmental agencies, political parties, and so forth. Is the word part of a name of a specific place or group of people? If so, capitalize it. If not, do not capitalize it.

A. Circle the letters that should be capitalized in the following sentences.

1. I am a new englander who was born in the south.
2. The hudson river separates new york from new jersey.
3. The islands of the pacific and the valleys of the appalachians date back millions of years.
4. He climbed mount everest.
5. The atlantic and pacific oceans are huge bodies of water.
6. The hudson and ohio rivers are important to commerce.
7. New york city is the largest city in america.
8. Kings county is in brooklyn.
9. Kansas city is well known as one of the largest agriculture centers in the west.
10. Purchasing agent jones has had many years of experience as a purchasing agent.
11. In the fall we have a large sale, which will be in november this year.
12. we would like your company to send us—the non-such company—a sample.
13. Secretary-treasurer Maria Sanchez dictated a letter to her secretary, bob smith.

14. The arrowhead hotel is situated on mount cisco road.
15. Easterners are not inclined to know as much about the west as westerners know about the east.

Trade names are protected by law and must be capitalized (*Plymouth car, Excedrin pills*). A few words started out as trade names but have been ruled by the courts to belong to the public because they have become applied to many products not made by the original manufacturer (*shredded wheat, aspirin*). Many of these words appear in your dictionary as lower case entries. If you think a word may be a trade name and do *not* find it in your dictionary, you are probably safe in capitalizing it.

A. In each sentence, cross out the small letters that should be capitalized. Write the capital letters above them. Write *C* if the sentence has no errors. Use your dictionary.

1. The best chinaware is imported from london.
2. Do you know that Pasteur discovered how to pasteurize milk?
3. He belongs to a society called the american association of publishers.
4. He studied mathematics, english, advanced algebra, and typing in school.
5. He was graduated from jefferson high school, but did not go to college.
6. My employer, carl smith, started the olympic printing company in the winter of 1964.
7. The plant is located in the southern part of south carolina.
8. After moving the plant to the mohawk valley, he became president of the printers association of america.
9. Mr. Smith then taught a course in english in Newark College for students with high school diplomas.
10. Carl likes to eat hamburgers and drink coca-cola.

The important words in a title of a book, speech, and so forth should be capitalized. Small words like *the, of,* and *and* should not be capitalized.

B. In the following paragraph, cross out each small letter that should be capitalized. Write the capital letter above it.

on wednesday, january 17, president james jackson delivered his winter message to stockholders of the apex screen co. in a speech entitled, "meeting the mosquito menace," he explained the firm's expansion into the northwest as part of man's never-ending struggle against the insect kingdom. calling for a "screen on every window," he demanded greater efforts in southern parts of the united states, where the mosquito problem was most biting.

UNIT 24

capitalization (3)

A. Draw a line through each letter in the following sentences that should *not* be capitalized.

1. The Popular singer Pearl Anderson sang the Song "Rocky Mountain Blues."
2. The next Solar Eclipse will occur 207 Years from now.
3. In the Spring of 1973, there was an Eclipse that could be Seen in Africa.
4. I will meet you on Tuesday of next Week at the hotel called the Morrison.
5. The Mississippi and the Missouri are Rivers of Great length.
6. Johann Sebastian Bach's "Easter Oratorio" was performed by the Great Conductor Bruno Walter.
7. The Salesmen omitted three Cities, mainly Spokane, San Diego, and Oakland.
8. "Tell me," he said, "Why I haven't Heard from you."
9. The director said: "The board will meet in the Month of April to hear the Treasurer read an Account of our financial position. This accounting should be attended by every member of the Staff."
10. The Apartments on 257 Woburn Street in Lexington, Massachusetts are completed.
11. Hampton, New Jersey is in the Western part of the state.
12. She said that the order "Had been received on the Previous Tuesday."
13. Santa Fe, New Mexico is in the Southwest section of the United States Of America.
14. A Department of Sanitation Spokesman said trash would be collected on Friday.
15. He came from a Department of Sanitation in a Western City.

Some people are in the habit of not pronouncing final consonants, particularly in words that end in two consonant sounds (*bend, effect*). Practice pronouncing *all* of the sounds in words.

The words that should not be capitalized in the titles of books, articles, and so forth are usually said to be prepositions, articles, and conjunctions. There are minor variations of this rule depending on the authority, but unless you work for a publisher or printer they need not concern you. If you do work for a publisher or printer, you will be able to find out the correct style for the material you will be working on. The first word in a title is always capitalized.

"The Walrus **and** the Carpenter"
"Yes Sir You're **My** Baby"

B. Circle the words in the following titles that should be capitalized.

1. the poverty of philosophy
2. all's well that ends well
3. the valley of the dolls
4. baby when the moon is shining is when i think of you
5. summary of new jersey's motor vehicle and traffic laws
6. the cayuga county reporter
7. the new york times
8. organic farming and gardening

C. Draw a line through each letter in the following sentences that should not be capitalized. Use your dictionary if necessary.

1. The Name of the Main Insurance Company's Policy is the Protection For Homeowners Policy.
2. The soprano Rose from her Chair and sang "The Last Rose Of Summer."
3. President Marco addressed the Presidents of several other Companies also engaged in the Food Business.
4. Our new product—the Lincoln Mercury—is, we sincerely believe, the best Automobile on the Market.
5. "I wonder," he said, "Why it has been such a long Time since Spring."
6. "I want to make it perfectly clear," he declared, "That we are prepared to go to War with all of the Far East if necessary."
7. The period between World War I and World War II included a disastrous economic Depression.
8. The title of the Vice-President's Report was "The Financial Condition of the Company as of April 15, 1973."
9. Mr. Castro, whose title is Vice-President in Charge of Production, gave a report on the Financial Condition of the production Department.
10. Our Company publishes many musical Compositions, including the "Song Of The Earth" by Gustav Mahler.
11. Shortly before the American Revolution, a Committee called the Committee of Correspondence was formed to protest British Policies.

namesectiondate

UNIT 24

capitalization (4)

Review

A. Rewrite the following letter capitalizing words that should be capital. The letter is continued on the next page.

mr. john murphy
17 lexington avenue
new york, new york

my dear mr. murphy:

    are you one of the many new york city businessmen who would like to spend a few days or a few weeks in the country, but whose business interests demand that you not venture far from manhattan? the hotel gramatan in the hills of westchester county, midway between the scenic hudson river and long island sound, offers you a most inviting home 28 minutes from grand central terminal, the heart of the shopping and theater district.

_____
_____
_____
_____
_____

The sound that begins *round* is spelled *rh* in *rhyme*, *rhythm*, *rheumatism*, and a few other words. The sound that begins *hole* is spelled *wh* in *who* and *whole* and in words made from them (*whom, wholesome*).

This is a continuation of the letter begun on page 209. Rewrite it, capitalizing where necessary.

   The hotel is of Moorish design, and the wide Spanish balconies encircling it are literally "among the tree tops."
  Accommodations are on the American plan, and the rates are considerably less than the cost of equivalent accommodations in town: single room and board, $50 per week and upward; large room and private bath with board for two people, $90 per week and upward.
  An excellent golf course, eight of the best tennis courts in Westchester County, a string of fine saddle horses, good roads for motoring and driving are offered.
  Walter E. Gibson, drama critic of the *New York Times*, visited the Hotel Gramatan in July of last year. Upon his return to New York, he wrote the following in his column, *Going On In New York*: "The Hotel Gramatan is one of the finest hotels I have ever visited. Its European cooking is tops."
  Why don't you take a drive up the scenic Hutchinson River Parkway and visit the Gramatan some time this fall?

         Very respectfully yours,

UNIT 24
capitalization (5)

Review of Punctuation and Capitalization

A. Rewrite the following letter with the necessary capitalization and punctuation. The letter is continued on the next page.

randall and peck inc.
35 draper avenue
rochester 10 new york

gentlemen

the enclosed booklet make your own weather will show you how to maintain your volume of business through the hot summer months read about our new scott portable cooler that will bring summer comfort to homes offices hospitals and hotels in your city it is an air conditioning unit that is both quiet and beautiful it is almost as easy to install as a radio and it can be moved from room to room and from building to building you cannot afford to overlook this opportunity

one large industrial user of the scott portable cooler wrote us as follows

This is the continuation of the letter begun on page 211. Rewrite it with the necessary capitalization and punctuation.

   our plant is located in the south where we face tremendous heat problems during most of the year we had considered installing other air conditioning units but all of them were too expensive then we learned about the scott cooler last spring we ordered one of the scott air conditioners for our executive office and were so satisfied with its superb performance that our purchasing manager was instructed to order scott coolers for the entire plant. I can't recommend the scott cooler too highly
  take the advice of this successful businessman and the thousands like him try the scott cooler
  to help our dealers we have arranged a demonstration at the factory on april 8 and 9 we invite your sales and service managers to attend this meeting at our expense.

             very truly yours

Learn to hear where the accent falls in words. Apply the rule about words with the accent on the last syllable when that syllable has a consonant-vowel-consonant pattern (*pin*): double the final consonant before a suffix beginning with a vowel. The past of *omit* is therefore spelled *omitted* since the accent is on the last syllable; the past of *edit* is *edited* since the accent is not on the last syllable.

capitalization (5)

abbreviations

As is so often the case in writing, your own dictionary is the best guide for reading and writing abbreviations. Find out where abbreviations appear in your dictionary, for in some dictionaries they appear in the body of the text—that is, *lb.,* the abbreviation for *pound,* appears after an entry beginning with the letters *la*—whereas in others they appear in a separate table, usually at the end of the dictionary (don't confuse the table titled *Abbreviations* with one titled *Abbreviations Used in This Dictionary*).

It is more difficult to find the abbreviation for a word than to find out what word an abbreviation stands for. You cannot, of course, memorize all of the following pages, but you might memorize the abbreviations for the states. You might also keep these sheets to use on the job. Few jobs will require you to use abbreviations in all of the categories given here, but you will find several of the tables useful. Which ones are most useful will depend on the nature of the business you are in.

States and Territories

The table below gives two forms of abbreviations as they are used to designate names of the states. Which abbreviation you should use will probably be determined by the nature of your position and by your company's policy.

Alabama	Ala.	AL	Georgia	Ga.	GA
Alaska	Alaska	AK	Guam	Guam	GU
Arizona	Ariz.	AZ	Hawaii	Hawaii	HI
Arkansas	Ark.	AR	Idaho	Idaho	ID
California	Calif.	CA	Illinois	Ill.	IL
Colorado	Colo.	CO	Indiana	Ind.	IN
Connecticut	Conn.	CT	Iowa	Iowa	IA
Delaware	Del.	DE	Kansas	Kans.	KS
District of			Kentucky	Ky.	KY
Columbia	D. C.	DC	Louisiana	La.	LA
Florida	Fla.	FL	Maine	Maine	ME

Maryland	Md.	MD	Oregon	Oreg.	OR
Massachusetts	Mass.	MA	Pennsylvania	Pa.	PA
Michigan	Mich.	MI	Puerto Rico	P. R.	PR
Minnesota	Minn.	MN	Rhode Island	R. I.	RI
Mississippi	Miss.	MS	Samoa	Samoa	
Missouri	Mo.	MO	South Carolina	S. C.	SC
Montana	Mont.	MT	South Dakota	S. Dak.	SD
Nebraska	Nebr.	NE	Tennessee	Tenn.	TN
Nevada	Nev.	NV	Texas	Tex.	TX
New Hampshire	N. H.	NH	Utah	Utah	UT
New Jersey	N. J.	NJ	Vermont	Vt.	VT
New Mexico	N. Mex.	NM	Virginia	Va.	VA
New York	N. Y.	NY	Virgin Islands	V. I.	VI
North Carolina	N. C.	NC	Washington	Wash.	WA
North Dakota	N. Dak.	ND	West Virginia	W. Va.	WV
Ohio	Ohio	OH	Wisconsin	Wis.	WI
Oklahoma	Okla.	OK	Wyoming	Wyo.	WY

Canadian Provinces

Alberta	Alta.	Newfoundland	Nfld.	Prince Edward Island	P. E. I.
British Columbia	B. C.	Nova Scotia	N. S.	Quebec	Que.
Manitoba	Man.	Ontario	Ont.	Saskatchewan	Sask.
New Brunswick	N. B.				

Days of the Week

Monday	Mon.	Wednesday	Wed.	Friday	Fri.
Tuesday	Tues.	Thursday	Thur.	Saturday	Sat.
				Sunday	Sun.

Months of the Year

January	Jan.	May	May	September	Sept.
February	Feb.	June	June	October	Oct.
March	Mar.	July	July	November	Nov.
April	Apr.	August	Aug.	December	Dec.

Compass Directions

East	E.	Northwest	N.W.	Southwest	S.W.
North	N.	South	S.	West	W.
Northeast	N.E.	Southeast	S.E.		

abbreviations (continued)

Units of Measure

Length

centimeter	cm.
foot, feet	ft.
inch	in.
meter	m.
mile	mi.
millimeter	mm.
yard	yd.

Weight

centigram	cg.
gram	gm.
grain	gr.
kilogram	kg.
pound	lb.
milligram	mg.
ounce	oz.

Time

day	d.
hour	hr.
minute	min.
month	mo.
second	sec.
year	yr.
before noon	a.m.
noon	N.
afternoon	p.m.

Electronic

ampere	a.
cycle	c.
kilocycle	kc.
kilovolt	kv.
kilowatt	kw.
megacycle	mc.
volt	v.
watt	w.

Standard Business Terms

abbreviated, abbreviation	abbr.
absolute	abs.
acknowledged	ack'd
acre	A
adjective	adj.
ad libitum (at pleasure)	ad lib.
administration	admin.
Administrator	Admr.
Administratrix	Admx.
adverb	adv.
advertise	adv.
affidavit	afft.
against	vs.
agent	agt.
agreement	agmt.
America, American	Am.
American Automobile Association	A.A.A.
American Bankers Association	A.B.A.
amount	amt.
and	&
and others	et al.
and the following pages	ff.
Anno Domini (in the year of our Lord)	A.D.
anonymous	anon.
answer	ans., A.
apartment	apt.
approximate	approx., ap.
article	art.
Associated Press	AP
association	assn.
at	@
attention	attn., atten.
Attorney	Att., Atty.
Avenue	Av., Ave.
average	av., avg.
Bachelor of Arts	A.B., B.A.
Bachelor of Science	B.S.
balance	bal.
bank	bk.
banking	bkg.
barrel	bbl.
Before Christ	B.C.
board	bd.
bill of lading	B/L
bills payable	B.P.
bills receivable	B.R.
bill of sale	B/S
Boulevard	Blvd.
branch office	B.O.
brother	Bro.
brothers	Bros.
brought forward	b.f.
building	bldg.
bulletin	bul.
bureau	Bu., Bur.
bushel	bu.

box	bx.	Doctor of Divinity	D.D.
by way of	via	Doctor of Laws	LL.D.
		Doctor of Medicine	M.D.
capital	cap.		
Captain	Capt.	each	ea.
carbon copy	c.c., cc	Editor	Ed.
care of	c/o	electric	elec.
catalog	cat.	employment	empl.
Centigrade	C.	enclosure	enc., encl.
cents	c., cts.	end of month	e.o.m.
certificate	cert., ct., ctf.	envelope	env.
certificate of deposit	C/D	equal	eq.
Certified Professional Secretary	C.P.S.	errors and omissions excepted	E. & O.E.
Certified Public Accountant	C.P.A.	establish	est.
		Esquire	Esq.
chapter	chap., ch., C.	et cetera, and so forth	etc.
charge	chg.	example	ex.
Christmas	Xms., Xmas.	exchange	exc., exch.
collect, or cash, on delivery	C.O.D., c.o.d.	Executor	Exec.
		Executrix	Execx.
company	co.	expense, express	exp.
collection	coll.	extension	ext.
Colonel	Col.		
commerce	com.	Fahrenheit	F., Fahr.
commission	comm.	Federal	Fed.
compare	cf.	Federal Bureau of Investigation	FBI
continued	contd., cont., con.		
copyright	©	Federal Communications Commission	FCC
Corporation	Corp.		
correct	OK	Federal Deposit Insurance Corporation	FDIC
credit	cr.		
creditor	Cr.		
		Federal Reserve Board	FRB
degree	deg., °		
deliver	del.	Federal Trade Commission	FTC
department	dpt., dept.		
dictionary	dict.	feminine	fem., f.
Director	Dir.	figure	fig.
discount	dis.	first	1st (no period)
district	dist.	first class	A-1
division	div.	folio	fo., fol., f.
direct current	d.c., dc	footnote	fn., ftnt.
ditto, the same	do.	for example	e.g.
dollar(s)	d., dls., dols.	Fort	Ft.
dozen	doz.	forward	fwd.
Doctor	Dr.	fourth	4th (no period)
Doctor of Philosophy	Ph.D.	free on board	f.o.b.
Doctor of Dental Surgery	D.D.S.	freight	frt., fgt.
		from	fr., fm.

abbreviations (continued)

gallon	gal.	International Business Machines	I.B.M.
General	Gen., Gen'l		
General Headquarters	GHQ	Interstate Commerce Commission	ICC
general mortgage	gm	inventory	invt.
goods	gds.	invoice, investment	inv.
Governor	Gov.	Invoice Book	I.B.
government	gov't	Island, Isle	I.
gram	g.	italics	ital.
gross	gr.		
guaranteed	gtd.	joint	jt.
		Journal	J., Jr., Jour.
half	hf.	Junior	Jr.
hardware	hdw.	Justice of the Peace	J.P.
Headquarters	Hq.		
height	ht.	karat	K., kt.
Highway	Hwy., Hy.		
history	hist.	laboratory	lab.
Honorable	Hon.	language	lang.
horsepower	h.p., hp	large	la., lge.
hospital	Hosp.	latitude	lat.
hundred	C	leave	lv.
hundredweight	cwt.	Ledger folio	L.f.
		Legislature	Leg.
		lesson	Les.
I owe you	IOU	let it stand	stet
illustration, illustrated	ill., illus.	letter	ltr.
improvement	imp., impr.	letter of credit	L/C
in the place cited	i.c.	library	lib.
in the same place	ib., ibid.	Lieutenant	Lieut., Lt.
in the work cited	op. cit.	Limited	Ltd.
inches	in.	line	l.
inclusive	incl.	list price	L.P.
Incorporated	Inc.	literature	lit.
industrial, independent	ind.	location, local	loc.
		longitude	long.
inferior	inf.	lumber	lbr.
initial	init.		
in regard to	re	machine	mch., mach.
insurance	ins.	Madam	Mme.
intelligence quotient	I.Q.	Mademoiselle	Mlle.
interest	int.	magazine	mag.
International	Int.	Major	Maj.
		Manager	Mgr.

manufactured	mfd.	page	p.
manufacturing	mfg.	pages	pp.
manufacture	mfr.	paid	pd.
manuscript	ms., MS.	pair	pr.
mark	mk.	pamphlet	pam.
market	mkt., mar.	paragraph	¶, par.
masculine	m., mas., masc.	parcel post	p.p.
Master of Arts	M.A.	parenthesis	paren., par.
Master of Ceremonies	M.C.	parkway	Pkwy.
		part	pt.
maturity	mat.	patent	pat.
mathematics	math.	payment	payt.
maximum	max.	per annum	per an.
medium	med.	percent	%, pct.
memorandum	memo.	piece	pc.
merchandise	mdse.	pint	pt.
Mesdames	Mmes.	place	pl.
Messieurs	Messrs., MM.	place of the seal	L.S.
metropolitan	met.	Plaintiff	Plf.
midnight	mid., mdnt.	population	pop.
military	mil.	Post Exchange	PX
miscellaneous	misc.	Postmaster	P.M.
Miss or Mrs.	Ms.	Post Office	P.O.
Mister	Mr.	postpaid	ppd.
Mistress	Mrs.	postscript	P.S.
money order	m.o.	pound sterling	£
Monsieur	M.	pound shilling pence	£s.d.
mortgage	mtg.	power of attorney	P/A
mount	Mt.	preferred	pfd.
municipal	mun.	premium	pm., prem.
		President	Pres., P.
namely	viz.	price	pr.
namely or to wit	sc., scil., sct.	principal	prin.
national	Nat., Natl.	private branch exchange	PBX
no good	n.g.	problem	prob.
not sufficient funds	N.S.F., N/S	Professor	Prof.
Notary Public	N.P.	Profit and Loss	P & L, P/L
note well	n.b., N.B.	pronoun	pron.
number	no., #	public	pub.
		Publishing, Publisher	Pub.
obituary	obit.		
obsolete	obs.	quality	qly.
opened	opd.	quantity	qty.
opposite	opp.	quart	qt.
optional	opt.	quarter, quire	qr.
ordinance	ord.	question	Q.
organization	org.		
original	orig.		
		railroad	R.R.
Pacific	Pac.	railway	Ry.
package	pkg.		

abbreviations (continued)

ream, room	rm.	subsidiary	subs.
receipt	rec't	Superintendent	Supt.
receivable	rec.	supplement	supp.
received	recd., rcd.	syndicate	synd.
reference	ref.		
Registered	®, rg., reg.	table	tab.
Registered Nurse	R.N.	tablespoon	tbsp., T.
regular	reg.	teaspoon	tsp., t.
Reply, if you please	R.S.V.P.	telephone	tel.
report	rep't	temporarily	pro tem.
returned	rtd.	Territory	Ter.
Reverend	Rev.	that is	i.e.
right	rt.	the following	seq.
road	rd.	the same	id.
route	Rt.	thousand	M
rural free delivery	R.F.D.	township	Twp.
rural route	R.R.	trial balance	T/B
		Treasurer	Treas.
		Trust, Trustee	Tr.
Savings	Sav.		
section	sec.	United Nations	U.N., UN
Senate, Senator	Sen.	United Press	
Secretary	Sec., Secy.	International	UPI
Securities Exchange		University	Univ.
Commission	SEC		
Senior	Sr.	very important	
school	sch.	person	VIP
shipment	shpt.	volume	vol.
signature	sig.		
signed	/S/	warehouse receipt	W.R.
singular	sing.	waybill	W/B
so, thus	sic	week	wk.
square	sq.	weight	wt.
standard	std.	which was to be	
steamship	SS.	proved	Q.E.D.
stock	stk.	wholesale	whsle.
Street	St.	work	wk.

Page 219